MOROCCO
Sahara to the Sea

M

MOROCCO
Sahara to the Sea

Photographs and Text by Mary Cross

Preface by Paul Bowles
Introduction by Tahar Ben Jelloun

Abbeville Press Publishers

New York · London · Paris

In Association with Umbra Editions

Jacket front: Bedouin boy atop the sand dunes of Merzouga, south of Erfoud.
Jacket back: Massive brass doors mark the entrance to the King's Palace in Fez.
Pages 2–3: The Erg Chebbi—the massive dunes of southern Morocco, stretching
toward Algeria as far as the eye can see.

ALSO BY MARY CROSS

Behind the Great Wall: A Photographic Essay on China - 1979

Egypt - 1991

Nan Richardson and Catherine Chermayeff, Directors

Umbra Editions, Inc.

180 Varick Street

New York, NY 10014

Designed by Thomas K. Walker, GRAF/x

The text of this book was set in Cochin and Trajan.

Printed and bound in Italy.

First Edition

2   4   6   8   10   9   7   5   3   1

Library of Congress Cataloging-in-Publication Data

Cross, Mary

Morocco : Sahara to the sea / photos and text by Mary Cross :

preface by Paul Bowles ; introduction by Tahar ben Jelloun.

p.   cm.

Includes bibliographical references (p. 238) and index.

1. Morocco--Pictorial works. 2. Morocco--Description and travel.

I. Title.

DT305.2.C76 1995

964--dc20   95-1266

CIP

ISBN 0-7892-0030-9

For Judith Rulon-Miller

A woman of rare grace, serenity, subtlety, and courage.
She has shared with me the brightest stars
that shine above the Atlas Mountains.

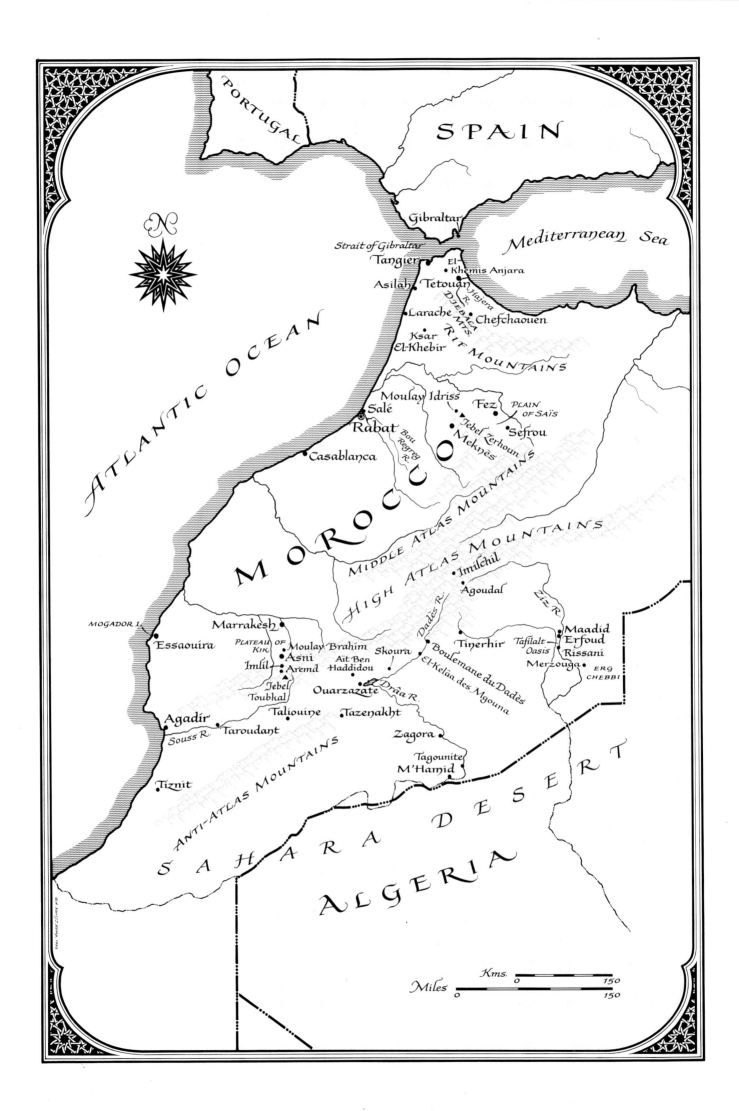

Contents

———

Author's Note

I am not moved by "photo opportunities." For the most part, monuments do not excite me—with the exception of the soaring towers of Chartres Cathedral, Luxor's Karnak Temple, the quiet majesty of the ninth-century Mosque of Ibn Tulun in Cairo, and a view of the Dome of the Rock in Jerusalem. What I cherish in Morocco, land of the farthest West of the West, are my memories of the people and the extraordinary beauty of the land.

To say that Morocco is visually beautiful is to say nothing. In a single day's drive, the traveler can experience landscapes that range from high mountain peaks capped with snow to hot, rolling sand dunes. I remember the drama of the high, black cliffs overlooking the rocky inlets and spray-washed beaches south of Rabat; the fluffy, feathery almond trees in delicate bloom along the Dadès River valley; a flower seller in Tangier's covered market who spontaneously presented me with a stem of creamy white tuberoses; a small boy in the blue-and-white, fairy-tale town of Chefchaouen rolling a hoop; and, on a cold September night, the stillness of the High Atlas Mountains as we slept in a tent, watched over by galaxies of fiercely bright stars while flocks of sheep trotted through our campsite, dodging tent pegs on their way to the next day's gigantic sheep market, ten miles to the north.

At dawn, I remember struggling up a dune at the Erg Chebbi, the site of Morocco's highest sand dunes. For every two steps I managed to climb up, I would slide one step down, knee deep in shifting sand. A young Bedouin boy dressed in blue patiently pulled and dragged me along like an unruly camel.

In the morning, as the doors of tiny shops opened in Fez, not tourist sights, but the view of urban Moroccans starting their day of buying and selling, caught my eye. And I remember Fez at night—the sound of Ramadan horns, and of drums passing through the twisted, medieval streets, the darkness before the dawn, the roof-top choir of a thousand roosters completing the early-morning calls to prayer begun by the *muzzein*.

I remember the elegant, though somewhat faded, structure of a tiled, public water fountain in Sefrou, a Moroccan man brushing his teeth from a water spout and rinsing his feet in the animal drinking trough filled with the icy-cold water that flows from the Middle Atlas Mountains. I cherish the sight of thousands of small, whitewashed, domed saint's tombs, or *koubbas*, serenely tucked away throughout the Moroccan countryside.

I carefully guard the memory of love and warmth that embraced me as I sat with a Berber family in the High Atlas village of Aremd: father and mother and five children all singing and clapping hands, laughing and swaying together, listening to a cassette tape of a popular Berber singing star. There are no toys in these simple households, but there is a remarkable amount of love.

MSC
Princeton
November 3, 1994

Children play hide-and-seek in the pale-blue streets of Chefchaouen, a town in the northern Rif mountains.

Preface

by Paul Bowles

Those who have been to Morocco are familiar with such official sights as Bab Mansour, the Menara and the Tour Hassan, along with others that are considered essential for photographic books dealing with Morocco. It is clear from the artist's approach to her subject matter that something more was desired than perfect likenesses of the better-known monuments. These are always there, in any case, ready to become postcards. The faithful, sensitive visual images in this collection supply an additional dimension, that of being wordless comments on their content.

A small fact, worthy of note, is the pronounced difference that can exist between the northern and southern sections of a given country. Germany has Bavaria, France has Provence, Portugal has Algarve, Spain has Andalusia, and even the United States has the Mason-Dixon line, fairly arbitrary as a geographical frontier, but very much in the public consciousness. In the case of the European countries, this difference in large part is a result of climate and its direct and indirect effects on the inhabitants.

In the kingdom of Morocco the forces dividing the country in two are fundamental and far-reaching. Indeed, here the contrast is strong enough to suggest two separate countries with very few elements in common. South of the High Atlas lie extensive regions where no form of Arabic is spoken, where race and culture are distinct from what is found in many other parts of the country, particularly in the lowlands and coastal regions. Islamization has been successful, but Arabization has yet to be accomplished.

Morocco is a country where the problem of remaining alive is the principal preoccupation. The faces of the rustic population, weathered by wind, sun and constant hardship, show what life is like. It is a raw land where necessities are not plentiful and where living is difficult.

The landscapes are startling; there are as many varieties as there are valleys. Far below the sinuous corniche, wide enough for two donkeys to pass, you can see the leaden Mediterranean. It is the land of the Aït Uriaghel, formerly pirates, now fishermen.

On the heights of the Middle Atlas, you watch the apes playing in the snow under ancient cedars.

And the tents of the transhumant Aït Atta are spread in the high meadows of the mountains. Beyond is the vast, flat plain of the eastern part of the kingdom, sometimes traversed by herds of camels.

There is a languorous breeze in the Djnane es Sebir, where the stream ripples through the willow leaves. The groan of the old waterwheel as it turns, never alters, never stops.

The door, pushed open, reveals the orange walls of the canyon, and to the left, the compact, mud village with the forest of date palms around it.

One lone *muezzin* calls the *fjer*, sending the fine arrow of his voice out into the darkness.

In the narrow village streets, young children play. They have faces like flowers.

It is one of the few happy accidents of the century that the period of European domination did not last long enough to annihilate the spirit or destroy the unique beauty of this extraordinary land.

Tangier
July 30, 1994

Introduction
by Tahar Ben Jelloun

Beyond the cities is the other Morocco. It lives in the red stone, in the sky swept by scudding clouds, in the eyes of men whose memories run deep. The other Morocco turns its back on the cities, though its men and women, made desperate by drought and want, may leave the mountain to lose some of their dignity in the wide streets of the asphalt towns.

The Moroccan population is largely rural, but many of today's city folk are yesterday's peasants and mountain dwellers. There is no frontier between town and country, not even a symbolic one. The lure of the city is strong, but despite everything, the mountain man, whether from the Rif or the Atlas, has not forsaken his roots. Even when he descends into the city, he retains his habits, his customs, and his language.

Ever since this other Morocco discovered the transistor radio and then television—run on bottled gas—the city has seemed much closer and far less mysterious.

But let us speak of beauty.

And of dignity.

Look at the eyes of these men and children in Mary Cross's photographs. These are people with dignity, even when times are hard, even when hope has grown feeble. A man in a white djellaba has stopped at the intersection of two alleyways. He stares at a wall. Perhaps he's considering his children's future. He is still, as if he were about to speak. Perhaps he is talking to the horizon. He is conferring with the red mountain, which he sees only in his mind's eye. He waits. He dreams, his eyes fixed on an arid land. This way of being, this casual stance is commonplace among Moroccans. What is he waiting for? Perhaps nothing. Just for time to pass. As he does, another man, perhaps a peasant, scans the disturbing blueness of the sky.

On a terrace, girls in their holiday dresses gaze out over the plains and mountains. They take pleasure in wearing bright colors. They enjoy laughter.

In the seventeenth century, the powerful Sultan Moulay Ismail built Meknès into one of the four magnificent imperial cities of Morocco. From there, he ruled for fifty-five years.

Another man, wrapped in a woolen *djellaba* and a burnous woven by women's hands, pauses a moment at his work. He is making brooms from reed cuttings. He lends his gaze to the photographer. He knows it is just for a picture, a snapshot. His gaze is just right. It is neither false nor mocking. It is the gaze of a man at peace with himself, of a man who has things to say. For now, he is keeping them to himself. This is the simplicity of profound silence. Wife and children are outside the frame. He is too modest to put them on display, at least while he is present. Intimacy is not for show. That is the secret of the mountain people. It needs no explanation. You open your house to a stranger; you show him respect by offering him the best bed, the best food, but you do not introduce him to your family. This is not hostility; it is modesty.

The water vendor has become a walking icon. He has remade himself in the image others have of him: his chest is laden with medals, brooches, little bells and a few talismans. He has become an object, no longer selling water but instead, selling the illusion of his job: He is there to pose for tourists in search of an exotic souvenir of the country. Bitter memory, soulless folklore. As for the three women draped from head to toe, they seem to have worn their haiks simply to harmonize with the bougainvillea and the blue sky.

The children of this bare earth are determined to live and survive by will and solitude. It is said that innocence holds little interest for them. These are not spoiled children. They are spry, rough with each other, and competitive with grown-ups. They do not play with dolls. They go to work at an early age in the fields and meadows. Little girls who lead the cows to pasture have no time to play with dolls. They have their dreams, and often, when their parents go down to live in the cities, they become little housemaids, exploited servants in the mansions of the rich.

These are not children like other children. Raised in adversity, they are harsh, without illusions about humankind. A stony bed, cold, hunger and hard work are their companions from infancy.

In town, they are employed as craftsmen's apprentices, market porters, car minders, and washers; they are shoeblacks and paperboys; they keep other people's places on line. Even when they are at school they hold odd jobs. These children of the Atlas are cousins of the street urchins of Rio, Bogotá and Cairo. Life has not been gentle with them. They know it, and soon learn to defend themselves and to rely only on their own will.

A young girl, a herder of dromedaries, wears a scarf on her head. This is not a veil, bears no relationship to those girls whose religion makes them hide their faces. In the Moroccan countryside, women do not wear the veil. They work as hard, if not harder, than the men. They toil in the fields and on the farm. They work all the time and rarely stop to rest. The men, however, take the time to live, to relax, and it is not unusual to see them on horseback while their women follow behind on foot. In this part of Morocco, the women are staunch—but no one speaks up for them. The feminist revolution has just begun to stir in the towns, among the middle classes, but it may never reach the countryside, ruled by ancient custom, unwritten laws, and traditions that grant few rights to women.

This northern woman (her red-striped blanket is typical of Tetouan and Chaouen) hunches over her basket, deliberately concealing herself in the dark shade from the photographer. The appropriation of one's image is disturbing to those who don't know where their photograph will end up, whose hands it will fall into, or what use will be made of it. They are suspicious. A picture is like a shadow, a tiny part of oneself, a transparency that eludes us.

In the southern Atlas, animals mingle with humans. The proximity is practical. Life is natural, basic, and above all uncontrived. Harshness is a part of everyday life. The lack of amenities doesn't seem to disturb anyone. They accept the vagaries of fate and the rigors of climate.

A publicity slogan from the early sixties boasted of Morocco's beauty in these terms: "In Morocco, nature is still natural." That was true at the time. Today, fruit and vegetables are no longer seasonal. They are available in stores all year round, like in Europe. Nature has been overtaken by the greenhouse. And the peasants have been overtaken in turn by industrialists from the city, applying methods and techniques that have made nature a little less natural than it was. In addition, the citizens have little respect for the environment. They've littered it with bottles and plastic bags, household trash and other things as well.

Despite all this, Morocco is still a country of peasants and craftsmen, whatever economic developments may have taken place. The great Hassan II mosque, built on the seashore in Casablanca, bears witness to the survival of traditional Moroccan crafts. For the ten thousand artisans who worked on it, masters and apprentices, it established the viability of their creativeness. The country has not abandoned its manual workers, its humble creators and anonymous artists. Plastic may have replaced porcelain and terra cotta; formica may have replaced wood, but there has been a return to traditional objects, to old-fashioned interiors, to forgotten ancestors and their way of living and entertaining.

When people say that Morocco is a bilingual country, they mean not only in its speech but also in its connection to modernity and tradition. It is just as comfortable in its traditional robes as in European clothing. In every instance, city folk are caught in the tension between two poles, two worlds. The results of this cultural "polygamy" are often deceptive. And yet, there is never at any time the kind of identity crisis that is seen today in Algeria. In that sense, Morocco is an old nation; its history is anchored in ancient times; it is the only country in the region to have resisted the Ottoman invasion. Berber and Arab, a Muslim people that has lived in harmony with its Jewish compatriots, Morocco strives to remain faithful to its past and worthy of its future.

The dyers concentrated in the Fez medina have been doing the same work for centuries. The same movements, the same application, the same tradition. They are often photographed for the vivid colors they work with and the bygone era to which they seem to belong. These are men who love their work, passed down from father to son, and who do it meticulously, in the open air, whatever the weather. Some tourists think they are just going through the motions to demonstrate how the art of dyeing used to be performed, the way the water bearer merely pretends to sell his wares to passers-by. But they are not pretending. These are artisans, faithful to their forebears, pausing every so often to pose for an awestruck photographer.

Some bakers continue to work in the old way, with wood-fired ovens. They bake bread for an entire neighborhood. The extraordinary thing is that they know the owner of every loaf and distribute each one without a mistake.

This Morocco is a place where all artifice has been swept aside, repudiated. The colors and contrasts have not been emblazoned on the sky and in the red earth to convince the travelers of its beauty and authenticity. They are there quite naturally. Men often look to the sky and hope that each year will bring enough rain. The winter of 1994 was generous. There is hope now that the peasants will remain on their lands and that the rural exodus, scourge of recent years following three cycles of drought, will be stemmed.

The beauty of the countryside is never flawed. It often exists as an endless dream, a burning passion, an utter clarity. And perhaps, with a little more social justice, a little more dedication to work, a little more common purpose, Morocco will achieve the perfect marriage between the most viable traditions and the most essential innovations. This opportunity depends on men, and not on the heavens. To bring together in one place all the contrasts of a civilization leaning towards Europe while remaining firmly rooted in its past and its history—that is the challenge the country faces every day.

Paris, 1994

THE PRE-SAHARA

The High Atlas Mountains divide Morocco into two sharply contrasting regions. While the northern area is favored by plentiful rainfall, excellent farming conditions, and serenely stable village society, to the south, where settled habitation is scattered and isolated, a sun-baked expanse of barren rock and sand stretches into the Sahara.

Like the spine of a colossal dinosaur, these mighty mountains extend through Morocco and reach across Algeria as far as Tunisia. In crossing this formidable barrier, dramatic changes occur. The spicy, winter scent of the spiky, green cedars and junipers whose aromatic needles fill the crisp, alpine-like air, are left behind. Tucked away in deep valleys between tall and desolate hills, a handful of tents woven from black goat hair, and belonging to Berber nomads, dot the vertiginous route across the mountain passes. Shy Berber women scurry single file across the winding roadway, bent over almost double under loads of scrub willow gathered for their cooking fires. In the spring, the nomads travel north to tend communal mountain orchards. In October, they descend to the valleys with their animals, looking for pasturage free from deep mountain snowfalls.

As the road leads south, the colors change. Terracottas, ochres, umbers, and warm pinks dominate the hot, dry landscape. Pockets of humanity become even more isolated from each other. Canyons and valleys provide sheltered areas of arable soil where water sources are naturally protected. These become oases, sustaining both human beings and their animals. This land, called the Pre-Sahara, comprises over one third of Morocco's geography. Closer to the Atlas range, the mountain oases of Ouarzazate and of the Dadès River valley are densely settled with Berber-speaking people. The oasis of Skoura (forty kilometers east of Ouarzazate) is an exception. Here Arabic is the first spoken language. Almond trees abound, interspersed with fruit trees—apple, plum, pear, and cherry— which cast their perfumed fragrance onto the warm spring air. Carpets of yellow, blue, and scarlet wildflowers spread across the valley. Olive trees provide a profitable harvest, while the roses of the Dadès are known throughout Europe and the Middle East. Each May, a huge festival of roses takes place in the town of El-Kelâa des Mgouna, attracting visitors from several continents.

Many women along the Dadès cover themselves with blue *haïks* (modesty cloths). The trim on the shawls—red and yellow pompoms and a bit of sequined glitter—bounces and sparkles as the women walk along the roadside, averting their glances from a stranger's gaze. Most of the women and their families live in one of a number of dreary, new settlements that have been built along the east-west highway.

Far more pleasing to the eye is a series of *kasbahs* that stand on the distant hills. The presence of these proud and lonely citadels, their crenelated battlements and their elegantly proportioned watchtowers—a bit crumbled but still intact—has enhanced the romantic reputation of southern Morocco, extolled as "the land of a thousand *kasbahs*."

Once occupied by fierce chieftains, *kasbahs* have lost their importance as tribal

---

Preceding pages: The crumbling, mud-red kasbah *(a fortification resembling a castle and usually belonging to an extended family), is a common sight on hills above the Drâa valley in southeast Morocco. Below the* kasbah *are lush, green palm groves that bestow a feathery softness to the riverbank.*

strongholds, but many are still occupied by descendants of these powerful warlords.

Flowing from the northeast, down through the mountains of the central High Atlas, the Dadès River forms one of the most extraordinary geological sights in southern Morocco. The deep valley has been described by travel writer Barnaby Rogerson as "a sabre cut in the High Atlas—a long, verdant riverbed surrounded by scarlet, scarred slopes. The brilliant range of red and carmine soils contrasts with a golden backdrop of denuded, treeless hills." On the south side of the Dadès the land is rich, supporting a large agricultural population. In the spring, clusters of women squat for long hours in the fields, cultivating barley, squash, onions, eggplant, and clover.

The longest river in Morocco, the Drâa, begins near Ouarzazate and flows south to the settlements of Zagora and Tagounite, near the Algerian border. Then the Drâa turns southwest, and the river, often a mere trickle, flows toward the Atlantic. The Roman naturalist and historian Pliny the Elder described huge numbers of crocodiles lining its banks a millennium ago; one of them, he said, ate a hundred men at a sitting.

Today in the southern oases, a poor date crop, water shortages, and severe unemployment have caused a massive exodus of males from the Pre-Sahara. These men have left the south to seek better-paying work in northern Moroccan cities, in Western Europe, and in the oil fields of the rich Gulf States. The remittances they send home—estimated at over two billion *dirhams* per year—are an important source of income to impoverished families across the country.

Throughout the Moroccan south, in every town and village, skin colors vary in degree from white to dark brown to almost black. The reasons for this can be traced to the history of the region. The Sahara itself sits on a huge deposit of fresh water. Most historians, geographers, and anthropologists believe that this vast, empty desert (whose wind-blown sands reach from Morocco across all of North Africa as far as Egypt), was once an extended green zone. Well-preserved skeletons and fossils show that lions, giraffes, zebras, and wildebeests roamed the plains tens of thousands of years ago. The green area that provided sustenance for animals also supported hunter-gatherer peoples whose settlements stretched from what is now Sub-Saharan Africa to as far north as the foothills of the High Atlas. Over millennia, the area grew increasingly dry. This climatic change resulted in scattered pockets of human habitation spread out in oases across the south, separated by miles of rocky terrain and dry desert. It is believed that most of the black-skinned population descended from the people who inhabited these oases.

A percentage of these very dark-skinned people were captured as slaves in the Niger Valley, present-day Senegal, Ghana, and the lands referred to as "Sudan" by North African chroniclers. The unfortunate captives were brought north by caravan to be sold along with gold, ivory, ambergris, ostrich plumes, and other exotic goods. These black people (called *Haratin*)—whether original oasis dwellers or of slave origin—lived under the authority of Berbers and Arabs who controlled the north-south trade, and who extracted tribute from passing caravans. In theory, slavery was outlawed in most of Morocco in the early part of the twentieth century, but it was not effectively eliminated until 1927.

South of Ouarzazate, the date palm is dominant and its harvest affords autumn many celebrations and great *moussems* (religious festivals). Dates constitute an important cash crop as well as a staple food in the southern oases of the Tafilalt and of the Drâa valley, where piles of honey-sweet, Mejhool dates lie in great profusion on the ground.

In the thirteenth century, a coalition of nomadic Arab tribes known as the "Maquil" brought the Arabic language to many people in the Drâa valley. These tribes remained the ruling power for hundreds of years. The seventeenth and eighteenth centuries witnessed the incursion of powerful Berber tribes who competed with the Maquil for control of the valley. Hence, the language of the southern desert and oases may be either Arabic or Berber. These sensible, southern oasis dwellers built *ksour*, fortified villages or towns, containing many families of different lineages. Constructed of dark, covered, tunnel-like streets rarely penetrated by even a ray of sunlight, a *ksar* (singular of *ksour*) kept out sand, wind, and heat. It was ideally suited to the harsh, desert climate. Despite poor ventilation and unsanitary conditions, many citizens of Rissani and nearby Maadid, both communities in Morocco's deep south, still choose to live in these ancient strongholds whose heavy doors are closed at night.

Perhaps because his proud Alaouite lineage originated in the palm-filled, southern Moroccan oasis of Tafilalt, King Hassan II affectionately compares his country to the desert palm: "rooted in Africa, watered by Islam, and rustled by the winds of Europe."

Fifty miles south of Rissani stands the beginning of the Sahara Desert. A four-wheel drive vehicle is the only practical way to approach the mighty dunes. Visitors often spend the night at small café-hotels on the desert's edge.

In the pre-dawn darkness, following a lonely track beyond Merzouga, lies a bleak wasteland. Rising spectrally from the empty, black plain is the silhouette of the Erg Chebbi—the massive dunes of southern Morocco, stretching towards Algeria as far as the eye can see. These impressive mountains of sand have stirred the muse of many Arab and Berber poets. The American expatriate writer, Paul Bowles, describes the experience of being in the desert:

> Immediately when you arrive in the Sahara, for the first or the tenth time, you notice the stillness. An incredible, absolute silence prevails outside the towns; and within, even in busy places like the markets, there is a hushed quality in the air, as if the quiet were a conscious force which, resenting the intrusion of sound, minimizes and disperses sound straightway. Then there is the sky, compared to which all other skies seem faint-hearted efforts. Solid and luminous, it is always the focal point of the landscape. At sunset, the precise, curved shadow of the earth rises into it swiftly from the horizon, cutting it into light section and dark section. When all daylight is gone, and the space is thick with stars, it is still of an intense and burning blue, darkest directly overhead and paling toward the earth, so that the night never really grows dark.

The city of Taroudant is enclosed by thick, crenelated walls of a brilliant, pink hue. Trailing masses of bougainvillea create a profusion of magenta. Fuchsia blooms abundantly. Before appearing in public, these women have carefully covered their faces and bodies with vividly colored haïks *(modesty cloths).*

The livelihood of this man of the desert depends on tourists who come to Merzouga to view Morocco's highest sand dunes. His base of operations is a coffee shop that is entirely surrounded by desert and bears the unlikely name Café de l'Etoile des Dunes. Visitors arrive before dawn to watch the sun rise. If they find dune-climbing too strenuous, they can hire this conveniently available camel to help them scale the mountains of sand.

Passing through the Drâa valley in southern Morocco, the traveler comes upon a dark-skinned people, the *Haratin,* who until recently, were employed almost entirely in agriculture or manual labor. *Haratin* means "those who plow the earth." They are a mixture of both a local black population found for centuries throughout the northern fringes of the Sahara, and descendants of the former slaves of nomads who were brought to Morocco from sub-Saharan Africa.

Outside the town of Taliouine in southern Morocco, this handsome, finely preserved *kasbah* was once home to the fierce and warlike Glaoui tribe. Now, in more peaceful times, it stands sentinel over the town, its square watchtowers ornamented with African shell motifs indicating the architectural influence of sub-Saharan Africa. The brown-skinned *Harati* peasant leading her sheep is almost surely a descendant of African slaves.

The features of this young woman from the Drâa valley show a mixture of African and Berber blood. Although no longer fashionable in urban cultures, the tattooed chin is still common among rural women. A girl may receive her first tattoo at age eight or nine. As she grows older, it will be enlarged until it covers most of her chin.

The most common tattoo is a good luck charm that guards against the Evil Eye. A simple line is drawn from the lower lip down to the cleft in the chin. More elaborate tattoos identify a woman's affiliation with her tribal family.

A few miles northeast of Erfoud in the sleepy, southern town of Maadid, the pace of life is slow and gossip is the principal pastime. Maadid is in the Tafilalt Oasis, a natural depression in the Sahara Desert fed by the Ziz River. The main economic activity is the cultivation of date palms in the lush groves that ring the town.

For Moroccans, the palm tree is a religious symbol and is protected by religious law. In the past, it was forbidden to sell a living palm tree. The palm is also a common fertility symbol; among country Berbers, the palm frequently appears as a tattoo on the hands of women.

This Berber woman is a native of the Drâa valley, and a member of the Aït Drâa tribe. Among the peasant folk of Morocco, there is a widespread belief in the exorcism of evil and in rites of purification. In May, the women of the Aït Drâa tribe walk ritualistically around the oasis of the Drâa valley scattering barley, henna, salt, coriander, and witch hazel. They circle the *koubba* (tomb) of the local saint, breaking eggs and leaving bits of the propitiatory substances. Thus, they entreat the spirit of their patron saint to give them *baraka* (blessings), to intercede for them in times of trouble and to protect their valley from the malign powers of the Evil Eye.

Maadid, in the deep south of Morocco, a few miles north of Erfoud, is home to two men who gossip in the warm March sunshine. One of them holds a palm frond that is used to chase away flies. Maadid boasts a fine *ksar* (walled town), that contains a maze of winding tunnels and a jumble of dark hallways that seem to have no exit.

A mother and infant, tightly shrouded in a pink-and-white *izar* (cloth), blend harmoniously with the warm pastels of Erfoud's painted houses. A tiny peephole around one eye permits the mother to maneuver through the town while she does the daily shopping.

In 1912, the Glaouis, a powerful Berber tribe in the southern High Atlas, became allies of the French. The fierce Glaouis helped consolidate the expansion of French rule south of the High Atlas. In the process they strengthened their own power and wealth. A chain of Glaoui *kasbahs* was constructed along the Dadès River valley. In 1953, cooperating with the French occupying forces, the Glaouis rose up against Sultan Sidi Mohammed Ben Youssef, forcing him into exile in Madagascar. When Morocco became independent in 1956 and the Sultan was restored to the throne, the Glaouis were humiliated and, owing to their collaboration with the French protectorate, lost all power and influence. They had indeed backed the wrong horse.

The rosy interior of a deserted Glaoui *kasbah* at Boulemane du Dadès boasts a beautifully proportioned courtyard flanked by columns on all four sides.

Handprints on the wall were to protect the inhabitants from the Evil Eye. But after the French withdrew, the handprints were not powerful enough to save the Glaouis. In the end, they were disgraced and their possessions seized by the government.

Preceding pages: The crenelated battlements of the *kasbah* at Boulemane du Dadès command a sweeping view of the countryside below.

The approaches to towns in Morocco are frequently graced by grand, often fanciful, ceremonial arches. The horseshoe, or keyhole, arch was developed in Spain in the eighth century. It became a hallmark of western Islamic architecture and is found today throughout Morocco.

This magnificent thirteenth-century example marks the entrance to the southern town of Rissani, located in the Tafilalt Oasis. Rissani is the birthplace or cradle of the Alaouite dynasty that rules Morocco today. The Alaouites are descendants of Ali and the Prophet's daughter, Fatima. The tomb of Moulay Ali Sherif, founder of the Alaouite dynasty, lies hidden away in the nearby desert.

Completely shrouded and veiled, a woman in the ancient, rosy-walled town of Taroudant in southwestern Morocco begs for coins. Giving alms to the poor is one of the five pillars of Islam. These are the fundamental precepts by which all Muslims live.

Overleaf: The town of Erfoud, painted a warm, reddish pink, occupies a huge oasis just north of the Sahara Desert. The variegated facades of modern housing incorporate elements of lively North African patterns and painted designs. But the streets themselves are another story: woe unto the child who falls into a hole in the pavement.

Between Zagora and M'Hamid in the Drâa River valley, this well-preserved Berber *kasbah* once provided protection from marauding nomads. The young man framed in the arched gateway claims to be part Tuareg, the renowned tribe of desert warriors of the central Sahara. The architecture of the *kasbah* is mud-brick, decorated with motifs revealing the cultural and architectural link between Morocco and sub-Saharan Africa. Similar wall designs are also to be found in Senegal.

Preceding pages: North of the mountain oasis of Ouarzazate, a large cluster of deep red, mud-brick towers rises on a steep hillside. The fortress is Aït Ben Haddidou, a village of several *kasbahs* packed closely together. Only six Berber families still occupy the crumbling *kasbahs*. The ruined complex stands on the bank of a gravel riverbed. This is the Mellah (Salt) River. When spring waters run high, a donkey or a mule can be hired for crossing, while in the early autumn, the dry riverbed can frequently be crossed by foot.

This scenic but fallen-down village was used in the filming of *Jesus of Nazareth* and *Lawrence of Arabia*. The sturdy and elaborately decorated gates near the river were built by the film company.

Overleaf: Seven kilometers north of M'Hamid, a Seven-Up sign provides the only color on a dusty road that leads toward the desert. Once an oasis for the trans-Saharan trade, this former trading post has become a drab and desolate village, but it is still known as the home of the "desert shrimp." These tasty morsels are, in reality, a kind of red locust that arrives in swarms in the barren desert nearby. Nomads collect sacks of locusts and eat them as a Westerner might eat potato chips.

M'Hamid is the last outpost before the Algerian frontier. Standing on one of M'Hamid's dirt streets and staring at the tan desert stretching away farther than the eye can see, the traveler may feel that he has, at last, reached the end of the earth.

A young Berber woman near the oasis of Ouarzazate.

In rural Morocco, many farm folk must carry water for great distances. Here in the Soussi region of southern Morocco between Taroudant and Ouarzazate, the family that occupies this adobe farmhouse is fortunate to have a well in their courtyard. A chicken shares the ledge with a black rubber bucket used for drawing water. These houses, made of simple *pisé* (mud reinforced with straw), contain almost no furniture. Thin mats and woolen rugs are used as bedding. Dogs, rabbits, turkeys, and goats all share living quarters with the family.

Overleaf: Every Moroccan village, however small, boasts of at least one mosque.

A merlon is the solid portion of a crenelated battlement, usually rectangular in shape. A more exuberant version can look like a Christmas tree. This variation is commonly found in Spain and Morocco on both contemporary and early Islamic buildings. These tiered merlons are believed by some architectural historians to date from ancient Mesopotamia.

In an Arab town, it is often impossible to distinguish the houses of the rich from those of the poor. The facades are closed and very simple doorways may lead to what may be spacious and elaborately decorated interiors. Windows are usually set above eye level and covered with grillwork, architectural lace mirroring the delicate fabric of women's veils. This doorway of a Berber house is akin to a *ksar*, and reveals nothing about what may lie beyond.

On the edge of the Sahara, surrounded by empty space, the Café de l'Etoile des Dunes presents a surreal image. At the edge of the great, golden sands, the tables and chairs are unoccupied.

In the evening, the café-hotel may be filled with adventurous dune climbers who will sleep on the roof, waiting for the stars to rise. Toward dawn, the stars will disappear, supplanted by a pale-orange, rising sun.

Overleaf: A family of Bedouin live in a black, woolen tent near Merzouga, the site of Morocco's highest sand dunes. The nomads raise goats who feed on the scanty scrub plants of the rocky desert.

South of Erfoud, in the southern Tafilalt at the site of a medieval *ksar*, the village of Rissani grew into a small but active market town. Rissani's *ksar* today is a maze of long, dark, confusing passages that lead into impenetrable blackness. Just as an outsider despairs of ever finding a way out of the labyrinth, a promising shaft of light may suddenly penetrate the gloom. Yet this light, too, may often point the way to but another dead end.

Living in terrible heat at the edge of the Sahara, the populace of Rissani is a blend of Arab, Berber, and *Harati* mixed with the genes of renegade Christian soldiers. Despite the heat, Rissani women swathe themselves in black from head to toe.

Overleaf: In Taroudant, a stark, modern addition to the nineteenth-century Palais Salam retains a bit of lacy grillwork and scalloped wooden awnings characteristic of old-world design. Once a pasha's palace, the Hotel Palais Salam is built into Taroudant's old city walls. The fanciful hostelry is a maze of keyhole gates leading into tiled courtyards ornamented with blue-and-green geometric patterns.

In Taroudant, a keyhole window draws the eye toward a hidden interior in the Palais Salam, whose walled gardens bloom with fragrant orange trees, bougainvilleas, oleanders, and hibiscus. Gurgling fountains and pools abound. In the palace gardens, there is even a murky pond filled with water turtles. In Morocco, turtles bring good luck and keep away the Evil Eye. It is also believed that the water from a pond where turtles live can heal flesh wounds.

The approach to Taroudant is rich with groves of citrus fruit: orange, grapefruit, and lemon. Bananas and olives also abound. Pink ramparts loom suddenly, overwhelming the eye with their thick gates and masses of flowers.

In the sixteenth century, under the Saadian dynasty, Taroudant became an important center in southwestern Morocco, trading in gold, sugar, saltpeter, and slaves. Through a deep gateway, a mother and child enter the medina (old section) of Taroudant. The opening is festooned with garlands of small, scalloped arches.

Although a major site of tribal warfare since the tenth century, Taroudant's four miles of crenelated walls have, remarkably, remained intact.

Wearing a blue cotton turban and robe reminiscent of the fabled "Blue Men" of North Africa's Sahara Desert, this young Bedouin stands on a high sand dune at Merzouga, south of Erfoud. His home is one of a small cluster of black, goat-hair tents that are surrounded by sand and a few scrub plants. There he lives with an extended family of grandparents, aunts, uncles, and a friendly collection of goats and dogs. His family owns one motorcycle, one camel, and one battered pickup truck. His father sells sparkling crystals and chunks of semi-precious stones: amethyst, blood-red wulfenite, and poisonous-green amazonite, fossils preserved in rocks from a local quarry.

Overleaf: March brings spring to the Dadès River valley, on the southern slopes of the High Atlas Mountains. Muddy rivers swell from winter rains and the runoff from melting snows. Almond trees dot the valleys and riverbanks, contrasting with the severity of the boulders that form the walls of the deep gorge.

MARRAKESH AND
THE HIGH ATLAS

The Berber city of Marrakesh dates back a thousand years, to a time when the Almoravids, a tribe of cattle breeders, moved north from the Sahara and set up their tents in the foothills of the Atlas Mountains. These desert conquerors, their origins in present-day Senegal, were zealous converts to Islam. Led by a powerful chieftain, Abou Bekr, and his successor, Youssef Ben Tachfin, the Almoravids established, about 1060 A.D., an empire that was to last a hundred years.

Under Ali Ben Youssef (son of Youssef Ben Tachfin) and the dynasties that followed him, Marrakesh developed into a powerfully fortified garrison town. The barely defensible wall of thorns that had once guarded the original tented encampment was supplanted by a massive rampart thirty feet high and five miles long. Dominating the city and the desert, the immense battlement of red earth and ruddy stone continues to be Marrakesh's most extravagant architectural achievement.

Protected by this great wall, the tents of desert tribesmen were soon replaced by early versions of the city's now-familiar, flat-roofed, red clay houses. Soon great *souks* and bazaars appeared, catering to the camel caravans from Timbuktu and present-day Senegal. Digging deep into the desert sands, the Almoravid princes built a massive system of underground aqueducts to bring the plentiful waters of the Atlas Mountains to Marrakesh and to irrigate the thousands of acres of palm groves surrounding it. A magnificent oasis city of cultivated gardens and cloistered beauty emerged.

In the middle of the twelfth century, the Almoravids in Marrakesh were overthrown by Almohad clansmen from the foothills of the Atlas Mountains. From their new base, the powerful Almohad sultans conquered southern Spain and established their rule over western Islam. The religious zeal and architectural gifts of the Almohads produced Marrakesh's central landmark, the minaret of the Koutoubia, known as the Bookseller Mosque, considered by some scholars to be among the most noble and beautifully proportioned mosques in the western Muslim world. So meticulous was the religious devotion of the Almohads that the original structure was demolished and rebuilt when it was discovered that the mosque was not facing directly east toward Mecca.

As the principal stopping point on caravan routes from Timbuktu to the Barbary Coast, Marrakesh became the El Dorado of southern Morocco, greatly enriched by the trade in gold, ivory, and slaves captured in the wars among the tribes of the Sahara. The city became the western terminus of a great chain of Islamic cities that continued from Cordoba, Seville, and Granada in Andalusia eastward to the cities of northern India.

Under the Saadian dynasty in the fifteenth and sixteenth centuries, Marrakesh reached its height of glory and became the golden capital of Morocco. In 1578 Sultan Ahmed El-Mansour ascended the throne as a result of his spectacular victory over the Portuguese at the Battle of the Three Kings near the Atlantic coastal town of Asilah. So important was this battle that later historians sometimes called it "the Poitiers of the Maghreb." The defeated Portuguese were forced to relinquish their trading centers on Morocco's Atlantic coast.

Preceding pages: In the wilderness of the High Atlas Mountains, women are free to come and go as they please. Two lone Berber women are traveling on foot through this wasteland of rocky hills. It is twenty miles to the nearest village.

To commemorate his great victory, Ahmed the Victorious built the glittering El-Badia palace in Marrakesh. The gigantic complex was to be the shining ceremonial heart of his court. Legend has it that the Carrara marble used in the construction of the palace was purchased for its weight in sugar. In 1602 the Saadian dynasty disintegrated and governmental power shifted to Fez. Today the El-Badia is a giant, empty ruin. Only contented families of storks nest on its crumbling battlements.

The ancient garrison town of the Almoravid camel breeders is now Morocco's fifth largest city. As of 1992, its population numbered about 600,000. Along with Meknès, Fez, and Rabat, Marrakesh is still considered one of Morocco's four imperial cities, yet it is no longer a commercial, diplomatic, intellectual, or political center. Nevertheless, Marrakesh remains a friendly, big-hearted city where Berber and Arab culture have met to produce a vibrant synthesis. Many Europeans and wealthy Moroccans come here to seek the winter sun and to be entertained. As a city of transit and trade to Timbuktu and the Sudan, Marrakesh remains distinctly African. Moroccan sociologist Fatima Mernissi, author of a subtle and sensitive account of Marrakesh, says of it:

> Marrakesh was the city where black and white legends met, languages melted down, and religions stumbled, testing their permanence against the undisturbed silence of the dancing sands.

Only two hours by car from the lush gardens and palm groves of scorching, sunbaked Marrakesh but a universe apart in custom and climate lies a great, glacial moraine of igneous rock. Here, in the central-southern High Atlas Mountains, the landscape is as rough and barren as the craters of the moon: no trees, no fields, no rivers—only huge, rocky hills and deep valleys hollowed out over the millennia. The road ends and those who wish to continue to the base of Toubkal, the highest mountain peak in the Maghreb, must continue by foot or by mule.

From a city that pulses with African drumbeats, ostrich plumes, and memories of camel caravans, the traveler is transported to a high valley of ice-cold, rushing waters, agricultural terraces, and earth-and-stone Berber villages built into ever-steepening hillsides. There is a feeling akin to being in the Himalayas rather than in Morocco.

The drive from Marrakesh is an easy three-quarters of an hour to the small, crossroads market town of Asni. On Saturdays, Asni is crowded with Berber men doing the week's shopping for their families. Hundreds of donkeys and mules are tethered near the market, waiting to be loaded with vegetables and other foodstuffs for the trip home.

A little past Asni, the road changes from tarmac into a muddy track of rocks and sinkholes. It winds past small, green fields neatly planted with spring barley. Low, stone fences carefully demarcate grazing land from that devoted to growing spring crops. Usually tended by the women, brown-and-white cows, gaunt and bony from a long, cold winter, browse contentedly in the valley pastureland.

The road rises toward the hillside town of Imlil following the serpentine coils of the powerful Asif Aït Mizaine River, which races down its cold, white path over wet rocks.

The currents of the river, named for a local Berber tribe, turn the wheels of a series of small grist mills belonging to various local clans. These granite grinding stones, operated by local women, mark the beginning and end of each tribe's fiefdom.

Even by four-wheel-drive vehicle, travel is not for the fainthearted in these, the highest mountains of Morocco. Winter rains and spring thaws produce rockslides, washouts, and crumbling roadbeds. Precipitous drops gape on both sides of the mountain track. As the road climbs ever higher toward the town of Imlil, Mount Toubkal, the highest mountain peak in Morocco (13,671 feet), comes into full view, although it is often wreathed in a halo of clouds.

Where the road becomes even steeper, uneven and treacherous, mountain people thoughtfully mark the edge of a sheer drop with small piles of stones to warn unsuspecting drivers of an avalanche or of a washed-out roadbed that may be awaiting them on the far side of a blind hairpin turn. Travel in the spring often entails fording streams and rivers swollen from melting mountain snows.

The village of Imlil has a few stores, some hostels for hikers and even a high school for the children from the many mountain villages in the valley of the Aït Mizaine. Here, in a huge lot, dozens of mules and donkeys, saddled and ready to go, wait patiently, available for hire by climbers and skiers. Beyond Imlil, a twisting new road built by villagers, supervised by government engineers, and finished in 1989, leads to the village of Aremd, a settlement of ninety Berber families.

Kaltumah Id Belaid is the fun-loving, lively, twelve-year-old daughter of one of the most prominent local families. She belongs to the tribe of the Aït Mizaine, who live in a valley of the western High Atlas. Like her older sisters, she is dutiful and obedient. She sweeps, scrubs walls and floors, runs errands, carries water, and pounds clothes on the rocks of cold mountain streams. Though not yet a teenager, she has already learned all the skills of keeping a house.

Kaltumah's parents own a few parcels of agricultural land in the village so, by local standards, the family is prosperous. In this region, girls are permitted to inherit land. If they marry outside their village they have the further right to sell any plot of land that they may already own.

Kaltumah goes to a local elementary school. Soon she will progress to a higher level in a different school four miles below in the settlement of Imlil.

After their work is done, Kaltumah and her sisters often amuse themselves by dancing inside their house to the recorded music of popular Berber folk musicians. When performed by young girls, the slow-motion dancing seems innately sensuous. Most traditional, mountain Berber women would never dance in front of men except on special occasions like marriages and *moussems* (religious festivals and fairs), when men and women dance together in rows or circles.

Even considering the relative prosperity of her family, it is likely that Kaltumah will marry a man from her village, maybe a member of her own tribe, or possibly a close cousin.

The rest of her life, Kaltumah will be busy giving birth, child-raising, doing all the family cooking and washing, and performing all the other household chores. She will spend most of her time in the company of other women in the village. On occasion, she will take a trip to a nearby city or visit a saint's shrine. After menopause, as a matriarch, she will be respected and will have a certain amount of independence and flexibility to move freely around the village.

Aremd has a history that stretches back at least into the seventeenth century. Each year at the feast of El-Khebir (celebrated seventy days after the end of Ramadan), village elders assemble and a storyteller recites a complicated, historical litany of ancestors and their deeds and a list of local milestone events: when each family bought land, who married whom, who died when, and the names of the children each father sired. The saga goes on for many hours. For these mountain folk, it underscores the importance and power of family continuity and tradition and the power of strong family bonds. There is a Moroccan saying: "A close family is like a scorpion; it holds you but it stings you."

As Moroccan Berbers combine pre-Islamic religious traditions with currently accepted Muslim practices, animal sacrifice is still practiced here on days of religious celebration, such as the opening of the plowing season. Another communal sacrifice, which takes place in August in the mountain village of Aremd, is held to placate Sidi Chamarouch, a mountain spirit believed by many to be King of the *Djinns*. *Djinns* are spirits who are present in both fire and water, and the belief in them is widespread among large numbers of Moroccans and other people in the Middle East.

Each August a festival, or *moussem*, is held in the nearby valley of the Aït Mizaine. Storytellers, traders, clothing salesmen, and doughnut bakers all make their way to this valley situated at the foot of Mount Toubkal. The valley is soon crowded with Berber families who set up tents and establish campsites in the green fields and meadows.

On the day of the sacrifice to Sidi Chamarouch, the King of the *Djinns*, the custodian of the shrine of the spirit is responsible for cutting the throat of a full-grown bull. The freshly spilled blood exorcises evil spirits. As the bull dies, the scene becomes a frenzied mass of chanting Berbers. As the bull staggers and falls to the ground, those possessed by *djinns* begin to wail.

Unstinting hospitality and generosity with food and shelter underlies all life in the High Atlas. You cannot visit a tiny shepherd's hut or a *caïd*'s resplendent quarters without your host's insistence that you enthusiastically partake in the ritual of drinking several glasses of highly sweetened mint tea. The ritual takes the same form all over Morocco, where many hours are devoted to the preparation and consumption of tea. Journalist Christopher P. Baker describes one such ceremony:

> …he measured green tea leaves flavored with sprigs of mint into a silver teapot and added boiling water from a kettle. Then he lifted up a large sugarloaf and using a special brass hammer, chipped off pieces of sugar until the brew became a strong syrup. With spare, precise gestures he lifted the pot so the tea fell a foot or more in a pale brown arc and splashed into a head of froth in each glass. He returned the tea to the pot and poured it out again with the same gestures. Then again. Finally, satisfied that the tea was sufficiently sugared and aerated, we drank the scalding brew, he with a loud sucking noise. After three glasses, the formalities were over.

The symbolic aspect of the tea ceremony was poetically encapsulated by Abdallah Zrika:

> The entire universe is contained in the teapot. Or, to be more precise, the sinia [the round tray] represents the earth; the teapot represents the rain; the sky is united to the earth by rain.

Nomads tenderly carry boxes of prized, etched tea glasses on lurching camels across the desert sands. It is said that in the stillness of the desert, the sound of the pouring of tea can be heard in the next tent. It is an invitation to come and share in the hospitality.

Traditional Moorish meals are equally ritualistic in their presentation and consumption. *Tajine*, a fragrant stew of steamed vegetables and sometimes meat, is a staple for both town dwellers and mountain Berbers and must be eaten in a particular and prescribed manner. While knives and forks have become more prevalent in towns and cities, especially in more sophisticated homes, in the peasant's world meals are always eaten with the fingers.

In the High Atlas, loud, appreciative smacking noises seem to be de rigueur when tasting soup. All diners sit on banquettes or on leather cushions around a low table. A steaming dish of piping-hot *tajine* is brought in, the conical lid is removed, and the container is set in the center of the table. The guest must serve himself that portion of *tajine* which is placed directly in front of him. There must be no reaching around to get a better morsel of vegetable or meat. Meat must be eaten last. All food is eaten with only the thumb and first two fingers of the right hand, which must be immaculately clean. If the guest were to use all five fingers, he would give the impression of greediness.

This Berber marabout (*holy man*) *is held by the local people to be a descendant of Muslim saints. Because of his stature in the community, he is believed to possess mystical powers. As he travels the roads, devout passersby stop to kiss his hand both as a show of respect and in hope that he will bestow* baraka (*blessings*) *upon them. His eyes are obscured by a self-styled headdress rarely seen in the Atlas Mountains. The tuft of hair just below his lip is called* dibbana (*fly*).

Preceding pages and left: In the *medina* of
Marrakesh at the aptly named El-Bahia
("the brilliant") palace, leafy shadows cast a
bold pattern on a shuttered window.
Throughout Morocco, this blue-green
color is common on doors and windows.
Moroccans are ambivalent about blue.
Its magical powers may either avert or cause
evil. The palace was built in the late
nineteenth century by Ba Ahmed, vizier
of Sultan Hassan I. The rich and powerful
vizier had four wives and twenty-four
"favorites." Arches and latticework
ornament the Courtyard of the Concubines.
The El-Bahia complex is a series of pleasure
gardens, shady courtyards, and elaborately
decorated rooms. A thousand craftsmen
from Fez worked for seven years on
the interior of the palace complex, decorating ceilings with exotic floral designs
and carving wood into fanciful scrolls and
arabesques. In 1912, under the French
protectorate, Marshal Lyautey, the first
French Resident-General of Morocco,
lived in the Bahia Palace on his visits to the
city of Marrakesh.

Overleaf: Northeast of the city of Marrakesh
lies the Jardin Majorelle, a lush botanical
garden originally created in the 1920s
by the French artist Jacques Majorelle.
After 1917, his watercolor paintings
were frequently used as posters to attract
French tourists to Morocco. His son,
Louis Majorelle, continued to maintain
and cultivate this immaculate and fanciful
two acres of plants, pools, and Chinese-
style pavilions.

This particular shade, known as
Majorelle blue, is the color of vivid morning
glories. Yves Saint Laurent has owned
the gardens since 1978 and his private villa
stands adjacent to the gardens.

A jumble of bikes is parked at the throbbing center of the city of Marrakesh in the Place Djemaa el Fna, meaning "the place of the last day of the world." The name derives from the many public executions held in this square by Moroccan sultans and caliphs as retribution for the plots and intrigues of their enemies. Today, this enormous, open area is crammed with vendors of every possible ware. Merchants sell their goods side by side with snake charmers, medicine men, storytellers, monkey trainers, palm readers, fire-eaters, acrobats, and sorcerers. All of these melt into a noisy, boisterous, good-natured mass that entertains both tourists and the local populace. The posters testify to the fact that American movies dubbed into French or Arabic are a popular import. Movie theaters are found in all large Moroccan towns and cities. The price of admission is about four *dirhams*, roughly 35 cents U.S., making films an amusement available to most Moroccans.

Throughout Morocco, sturdy donkeys are the preferred beasts of burden. In Marrakesh, a young boy drives a cart through the streets carrying the remains of dead animals that will be converted into unknown products.

Six-pointed Stars of David ornament an ancient door in the Jewish quarter of Marrakesh. The quarter was officially created in 1558 by Abdullah El-Ghalib, a Saadian sultan. The practice of ghettoizing Moroccan Jews in defined sections of Moroccan cities, called *mellahs* ("places of salt"), originated as early as the thirteenth century. Some *caïds* (town fathers) argued that the act of separation was a benevolent safeguard to protect the Jewish populace from persecution by their Muslim neighbors. The term *mellah* was said to derive from the fact that Jews were assigned the gruesome practice of draining and salting the heads of decapitated rebels before impaling them on the gates of the town. Throughout the country Jews were required to wear black clothes and black shoes or slippers. Forced to walk barefoot in front of all mosques, Moroccan Jews were also forbidden to ride on any animal or any other means of conveyance. In the royal cities of Fez, Meknès, and Marrakesh Jews were not even permitted to wear shoes, no matter where they walked.

The familiar six-pointed Star of David was also an old Berber motif and is still found today in the tribal design of rugs woven in the western High Atlas Mountains.

Hoping to rival Fez as an intellectual center, the *Madrassa* of Ben Youssef was established by the Merinids in the fourteenth century and was rebuilt in 1564 by the Saadian sultan Moulay Abdallah. Students from all over the country came to Marrakesh to study for a six-year period, memorizing the *Qur'an* and studying religious law. Over one hundred small, sparse student rooms were arranged around a series of internal lightwells, each embellished with a handsome, carved wooden balcony. The *Madrassa* is known for its great harmony and simplicity of design.

The custom of selling the scarce and prized commodity, water, seems to produce an uneasy contradiction in a country where, for millennia, water has been community property. The clanging of a large brass bell announces the approach of a *garrab* (waterman), who is a relic of days gone by. Exchanging water for a few coins or goods in local markets or public squares, these men were a time-honored institution in medieval Morocco. The multicolored hat fringed with dangling tassels is of a style still found in the Zemmour area between Fez and Rabat. With brass and copper cups hanging heavily from their clothing, the elaborately costumed watermen are now found only in parts of Morocco that are frequented by tourists.

These two sisters, residents of the High Atlas Berber town of Imilchil, are in the nebulous period between childhood and adulthood. In three or four years, they will begin to wear heavy silver jewelry, necklaces strung with enormous amber beads, and elaborate, tasseled headdresses. They will rouge their cheeks and lips with honey and coral cochineal and begin to outline their eyes with *kohl*, rendering themselves both available and desirable for the marriage market. The membership of these girls in the Aït Haddidou tribe is indicated by the indigo cross-hatched tattoo that starts at the lower lip and continues down the chin. In some Berber tribes tattoos are made more elaborate as the young women grow older.

Preceding pages: The lush Plateau of Kik is located west of the holy town of Moulay Brahim in the foothills of the western High Atlas Mountains. The plateau has few visitors because only a dirt track traverses the densely vegetated plain. Here, as everywhere in Morocco, the women are responsible for gathering animal fodder. This huge, fertile plain produces green barley and wheat. Wild mustard, orange poppies, and painted daisies peek through the barley stalks. Five tiny limestone villages dot the verdant plateau. The most memorable landmark on the vast plain is a twelfth-century Almohad fortress, once a defense against mountain marauders.

Imilchil, a Berber town in the central High Atlas, is renowned for its annual three-day betrothal festival, held nearby in mid-September. Young men and women from the Aït Haddidou tribe meet in a sanctioned community ritual. As many as thirty single and eligible men, all dressed in white, register with town officials announcing their availability as prospective husbands. Virgin girls, filled with hope and promise, arrive in town chaperoned by their families. An element of pathos is introduced by the presence of widows clinging to the often remote dream of remarriage. Widows hold a terribly marginalized position in Berber society, and their economic position is precarious. Divorcées fare better. Some may discard their husbands and acquire new ones each year. This seemingly casual practice bears no stigma. All prospective brides wear traditional woolen cloaks, striped in red, purple, and green. The young, unmarried women cover their hair with a scarf over which is placed a rounded headdress embellished with spangles and tassels. Widows and divorcées can be distinguished by their pointed bonnets. In the Moroccan countryside, men and women unrelated by blood or marriage do not meet publicly or interact personally. Ordinarily, the slow, rhythmic dancing that follows the initial flirtation sanctioned at the local festival would be condemned by Moroccan taboos.

Among the Berbers of the High Atlas Mountains, time-honored traditions are immutable. A married woman must maintain "modesty" at all times. She may not show herself before any man who is neither a relative nor an extraordinarily close and intimate friend who is considered to be a family member. If any other adult male comes for a visit or a meal, the wife in the Berber household will prepare food, then hand the hot, cooked meal to her husband to serve. In the simple Berber houses of the High Atlas Mountains, kitchens are invariably dark and are usually ventilated by a single window. In warm weather, cooking is done on an outside terrace. In winter, the children, especially daughters, spend hours in the smoke-filled kitchens, happily snuggling close to their mothers. The older girls assist in the preparation of meals. Mother-daughter relationships are invariably loving and affectionate.

In the western High Atlas, Jebel Toubkal, Morocco's highest peak, is known as "the mountain of mountains." At the foot of this great, snow-covered mountain lies the small Berber village of Aremd. Here the girls and women are unusually beautiful. Their eyes are set wide apart and their rosy complexions are without blemish. The babies, too, have bright, rosy cheeks, and the little girls wear their thick, curly hair in top knots. It is understood that big sisters will look after their small sisters and brothers. This young girl, Hadisha Id Belaid, carries her small cousin on her back. Everywhere in Morocco, warmth and tenderness in family relationships abound. The celebrated Moroccan sociologist, Fatima Mernissi, describes Moroccan family relationships as full of *hanan*, "a free-flowing, easy-going, unconditionally available tenderness."

In the High Atlas village of Aremd, preparation of a loom is a cooperative effort involving many women all belonging to a complex, extended family embracing three generations. This loom will produce a wool blanket woven in vibrant hues. It is also the responsibility of women to weave men's clothing. Most of the men go to Asni or Marrakesh to shop, but only the most prosperous can afford store-bought clothes.

Among members of the Aït Mizaine tribe, women's work is unremitting. In addition to weaving, they are responsible for child rearing and preparation of all food for the household, assisted by any unmarried daughters who remain at home. Grown daughters still at home have poor prospects of finding a husband. While helpful in sharing chores, their presence means another mouth to feed, and there is a certain social stigma attached to having an unmarried girl. Walking from their houses to the bottom of a steep hill, Aït Mizaine women wash clothes in the icy water of a mountain stream. (In September the water is warm enough for swimming.) They then retrace their steps, carrying heavy bundles of wet wash on their heads. The women also assist the men in weeding and harvesting crops. Furthermore, women not only take the cows and goats to pasture but also milk them and make butter and cheese. At the end of the day, Aït Mizaine women cook the evening meal, clean all the dishes, and fall into bed, exhausted. In the morning they will be the first to rise in order to start the fire and prepare breakfast.

Kaltumah Id Belaid, the twelve-year-old daughter of a prominent local family, carries water for her mother.

At the great September livestock market in Imilchil, the sheep are tied together, twenty to a bunch, for ease of selling and efficiency in packaging. Fastened head to head, the alternating pattern results in a pleasing, geometric symmetry. Moroccans do not crop the tails of their sheep. Unruly goats are moved about by their hind legs, wheelbarrow style. The trading is solemn and in deadly earnest. There is a fervor and intensity to the negotiations. Most of the proffered sheep are sold by midmorning. The shepherds now have money to buy clothes, teapots, aluminum cookware, and plastic pans, all available in great abundance at the market. The Imilchil *souk* even boasts a cheery dentist who exhibits jars of teeth he has extracted and a tray full of dental tools that look like pliers.

Overleaf: For the Berber shepherd tribes of the valleys, the September *moussem* is the most important market of the year. Early mountain snowfalls will soon cover the villages of the High Atlas, isolating them for many frozen, lonely months. By selling some of his flock, a shepherd can provide himself with necessary supplies and factory-made goods for the winter. In Imilchil, the sale of a healthy young sheep will fetch U.S. $27. On the eve of the great market, double-decker trucks loaded with sheep and goats rumble into Imilchil, and the owners set up their tents for shelter. Less prosperous shepherds drive their flocks on the hoof for long distances over rocky hillsides into the center of town. They arrive at the market site before daybreak.

Right: These Imilchil Berbers, whose dialect is Tamazight, discuss the upcoming market, where a year's supply of wool, grain, vegetables, and meat will trade hands. To the right stands the granary of the settlement, a building traditionally used for protection against all marauders, where the town's winter food supply will be housed.

Preceding pages: The semi-nomads who live 250 miles south of the imperial city of Fez move into the dry, southern slopes of the eastern High Atlas Mountains in the summer, but always return to the same valleys in the fall. Their camels are laden with black, woolen-fringed tents, live chickens, cooking pots, tent poles, and other necessities. Women are responsible for setting up the tents and taking them down when camp is struck. In the semi-nomadic culture there is a proverb: "A woman is the ridgepole of the tent."

Seen from inside the new Glaoui *kasbah* (1934–55), a lacy grillwork frames a view of the gardens and planted fields that surround the ruins of the nineteenth-century Glaoui tribal fortress of Telouèt.

The newer fortress, built by Caïd Brahim, is layered with towers, crenelations, and buttresses. Now stripped of carpets and furniture, it stands empty and decaying. Its cavernous rooms still retain their ornate, wooden ceilings, which echo the lonely footsteps of the occasional visitor.

For Moroccans, Telouèt is a monument to the treason of the Glaoui tribe, which from 1912 until 1956 aligned its fortunes with the despised French colonial protectorate. With the restoration of the monarchy and the defeat of the French, most Glaouis lost all power and influence. Disgraced and humiliated, many ended their days in prison. There has now been a certain upswing in their fortunes. In the 1970s, Abdessadeq El-Glaoui, a direct descendant of the opportunistic pasha of Marrakesh, Thami El-Glaoui, was appointed Moroccan ambassador to Washington by King Hassan II. The *kasbah* of Telouèt stands a few miles east of the windswept and heart-stopping Tizi-n-Tichka Pass (whose summit reaches 2,260 meters), which crosses the High Atlas on the road from Marrakesh to Ouarzazate.

What to the unknowing city dweller looks like a charming bouquet of wild poppies carefully chosen for beauty, color, and form is in fact the result of an hour of careful weeding by a Berber girl. One of her responsibilities is to dig out offending wildflowers threatening to choke her family's crop of ripening wheat. In Moroccan cities and towns, beauty masks made from spring poppies are highly valued as nourishing facial treatments. The petals and pollen are collected from the scarlet flower, lemon juice is squeezed over the petals, and the mixture is left to soak for several days. A soft paste results, which is applied to the face and allowed to dry.

In the high mountain village of Aremd,
Hadj Mohammed, patriarch of the Id Belaid
family, sips juice on his son's outdoor
terrace. The house is adjacent to an enclosed
and sanctified religious ground. Mohammed
Id Belaid has received the honored title
of *Hadj* (one who has made the pilgrimage
to Mecca). He also holds the important and
lucrative position of keeper of the *koubba*
of Sidi Chamarouch. This shrine, a two-hour
walk from Aremd, is venerated by the local
Berbers and many other mountain people.

Spring has arrived in the Aït Mizaine valley near the foot of Mount Toubkal. The cherry trees, which provide a cash crop for the villagers of the valley are in full bloom. Early green sprouts of barley and pumpkin decorate the tiers of the distant agricultural terraces. Here, not far from the tiny mountain village of Fimlil, two young brothers tend the family's baby goats. If one approaches nearer, patches of ringworm can be seen on the heads and cheeks of the young boys. Ringworm is an affliction common to children in the High Atlas.

Overleaf: It is washday in the village of Fimlil. Conveniently situated balconies and terraces are used for drying the day's laundry. The women and teenage girls have carried the laundered clothes, along with the hand-woven, multistriped blankets, from the riverbank far below. Unless a donkey or cow is available for transport, women carry the heavy pans of wet laundry on their heads. Carved into the side of the mountain, this Berber village is reached by a narrow road that winds its tortuous way from Imlil to Aremd. The stone houses and agricultural terracing are characteristic of dwellings in the western High Atlas. Communal pastures and small, privately owned agricultural plots, delineated by low, stone walls, occupy the few flat areas of the valley.

Right and overleaf: On a March morning following the end of the holy month of Ramadan, the highest mountain peaks of Jebel Toubkal are obscured by a heavy cloud cover. On this feast day, when all fasting has been completed, Berber men of the High Atlas village of Aremd gather for a sermon and communal prayer in a small, sanctified enclosure at the foot of the great mountain. The sermon is delivered by a *faqih* (a *Qur'anic* teacher and leader in prayer), who comes from another village some kilometers down the hill. Following these observances, the men form a single-file procession across the meadows to the village mosque, where they will pray once more. They will then join their families for a long-awaited meal of couscous and *tajine*, (a rich stew of vegetables). Meat is expensive and is not often served by mountain folk. But today there will be lamb in the *tajine*.

On the blessed morning following the end of Ramadan, alms of dried fruit, nuts, and grain are given to the poor. At this most holy time, ritual prayers are offered throughout Morocco—in tiny villages as well as in large, urban areas.

Although Moroccans often display an intense individualism, they are unfailing followers of Islam, a religion that requires the submerging of strong individual wills into a community of believers who abandon themselves to the will of God.

Preceding pages: Because all of Islam is celebrating the feast day of *Id el-fitr* (the day of breaking the fast), these Berber girls and women are taking a welcome respite from the unending toil of their normal lives. They stand on a housetop terrace watching their menfolk gathered below in communal prayer. After prayer they will listen to a sermon commemorating the end of the holy month of Ramadan. Because it is a special feast day, many of the women are wearing new clothes. In Aremd, as in other remote Berber villages of the High Atlas, some women are lucky enough to own a flickering, battery-run television. They often watch Egyptian soap operas, which provide a diversion from their arduous labor. Otherwise, feast days and special events such as weddings are the only break in their dreary routine.

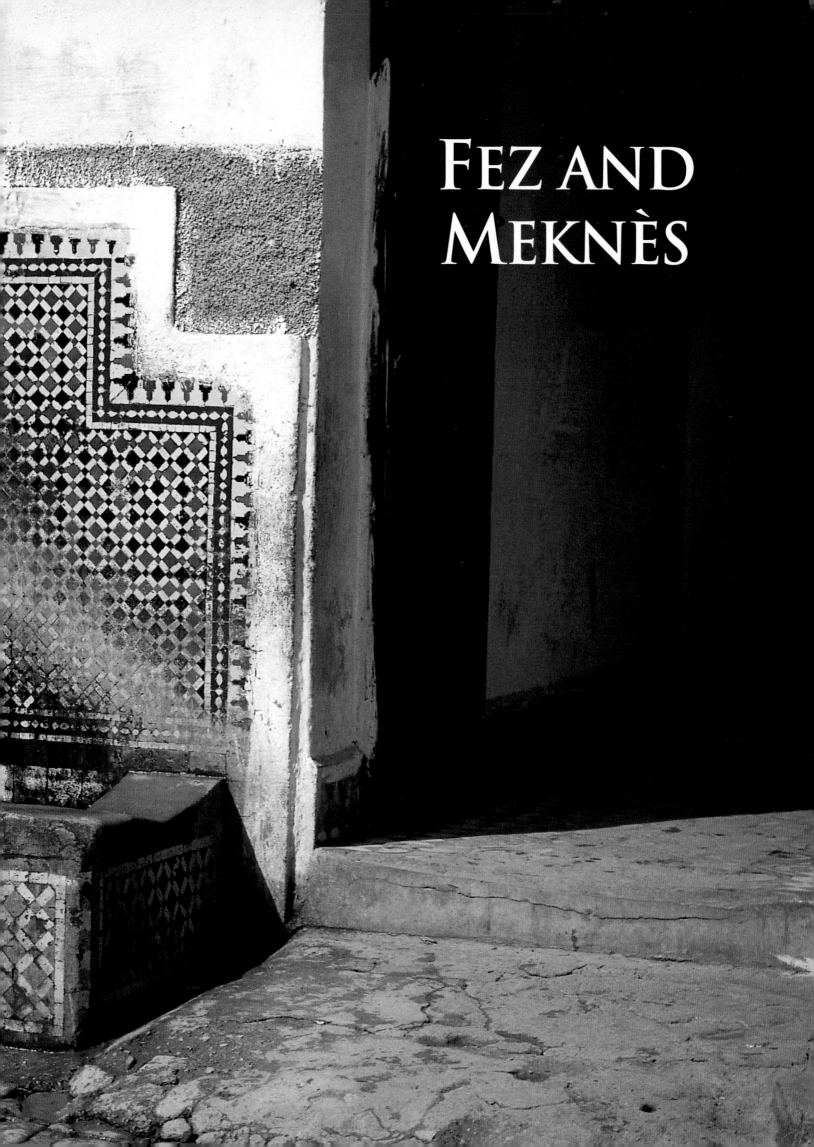

FEZ AND MEKNÈS

Under a warming March sun, the drive from Casablanca to Fez takes the traveler through a rolling countryside resplendent with brilliant squares of color. Cultivated mustard, a vivid yellow, and fields of *jimira,* the intense color of orange marigolds, create a startling quilted design contrasting with fields of early, green barley. Frothy wild mustard takes root freely anywhere and everywhere, in the crevices of tumble-down stone walls and even between the tiles on rooftops. Morocco is full of such unplanned gardens.

Next to thorn bushes and prickly pears, mimosa trees grow abundantly, their pendulous branches laden with fragrant, golden blossoms like small, fuzzy yellow explosions. The road continues past groves of tall cork trees, which are stripped of their useful bark every seven years. Their thin trunks, painted white to protect them against invading insects, resemble the slender, tape-bound legs of thoroughbred horses before a race.

Gray-green olive trees planted in tidy, curved rows follow the contours of the gentle hills, their round shapes reminiscent of the trees in a children's picture book. Along the roadside, Berber farmers offer plump chickens and turkeys for sale. Destined for a pot of Moroccan stew, or *tajine,* and staked to the ground, they do not even flap their wings or attempt to escape their sure and certain fate. Empty, recycled water bottles hold fresh eggs ready to be sold, and in the dry fall season, when the colors of the hills turn from brilliant green to mauves and ochers, sacks of almonds can be bought at bargain prices at the open-air markets.

Fifty years ago, English travel writer Nina Epton wrote in romantic prose:

> Fez is ancient and noble, a voluptuous and subtle charmer, overpowering the soul, lulling one's senses with the poison. Here there is no sense of time and space. Here magic carpets are woven, love philtres are brewed, magicians and sorcerers stalk through narrow winding streets to disappear suddenly as through enchantment into the recesses of those white walls. No one can spend a night during Ramadan under the moonlit ramparts of Fez, submitted to the aphrodisiacal influence of Arab music, and still remain entirely European.

Excessive Orientalism aside, to pass a night inside the ancient medina of Fez during Ramadan still conjures up medieval enchantments. Ramadan horns, often several feet long, sound throughout the night, sending forth long, deep, woody sustained notes that sound extraordinarily like the hoarse trumpetings of bull elephants. Through the dark streets, drummers accompany the horn blowers, beating a steady tattoo on animal skins stretched tight over terra-cotta drums. As the small processions weave their way through the tangled streets of the old city and plunge into deep labyrinthine passages, their music becomes muted and transformed.

The plaintive cries of the *muezzin,* lifting their voices in contrapuntal sequences, awaken the city in the hours before dawn. The first exhortation to prayer begins at the

---

Preceding pages: Most Moroccan communities include a hammam *(Turkish bath), a mosque, a Qur'anic school, a communal bakery, and a public fountain. This richly decorated fountain was built by a wealthy Sefrou family to provide water to city dwellers. Melting snows from the Middle Atlas Mountains provide Sefrou with an unlimited supply of icy cold, pure water. Many inhabitants of Sefrou's medina have no indoor plumbing and must rely on public water supplies.*

Karouine Mosque. Soon a second, third, and then hundreds of *muezzin* are crying out from minarets higher up the hill of the old city, their voices blending and intertwining in haunting polyphony. "Prayer is better than sleep," they admonish. There is great comfort in the sound. The continuity of thirteen hundred years of unshakable faith is embodied in the calls of the *muezzin*. Drums beat, music throbs, the city does not sleep.

According to Muslim tradition, it is only when one can distinguish a white thread from a black thread that a veil of silence falls for a brief time upon the gray limestone city of Fez. In the breaking light, the city takes on the delicate fragility and luminescence of a faded moth wing.

Once known as the Athens of North Africa, Fez is the oldest of Morocco's four imperial cities. It remains today a medieval city fundamentally unchanged. Fez was founded in 789 by Moulay Idriss, a kinsman of the Prophet Mohammed. In less than one generation, it grew from a tiny Berber settlement into a distinctly Arab town from which the Arabic language, religious scholarship, and technical knowledge filtered out into the hinterlands to Arab and Berber alike. Seventy-five years ago Walter Harris, the English journalist and companion of sultans, wrote:

> No Sultan can count upon his throne as being safe until he has been accepted by the religious and aristocratic Fezzis, and taken up his residence in the city; for Fez is the centre of religion and learning—and also of intrigue—and the influence of its population upon the tribes is very great.

In A.D. 818 a civil war in the Arabized Spanish state of Andalusia brought eight thousand refugees pouring into Fez. This enormous tide of Spanish Muslims settled on the east bank of the Fez River. The Andalusians brought a degree of urban sophistication to the city, along with a heritage of vigor and bravery. The Andalusian women were reputed to be the most beautiful in the western Mediterranean. A mere seven years later, another wave of refugees arrived in Fez. This time it was the Karouines from the area that is now modern Tunisia. The new arrivals were rich craftsmen and merchants, long accustomed to a comfortable and prosperous city life. Settling on the opposite bank of the river, they were elegant and well-educated, with a distinct penchant for sybaritic pleasures. Fez thus became two separate cities, each surrounded by a high wall and divided by the fast-moving waters of the River Fez (known also as the River of Pearls).

In 1069 Almoravid Sultan Youssef Ben Tachfin, the leader of a puritanical Almoravid Berber dynasty, conquered Fez and constructed a crenelated wall uniting the two settlements into a single defensive unit. Thus the Almoravids succeeded in melding an integral Islamic state from the confusing welter of Arab trading towns, warring Berber tribes, and intrusive foreign garrisons.

The glittering zenith of Fez's architectural and intellectual history came two hundred years later during the ascendancy of the Merinids, nomadic Berbers from the eastern plains, who conquered the great Islamic town and firmly established it as the capital of Morocco. Merinid tombs still dot the olive-treed hills overlooking the city.

Under the Merinid dynasty, dozens of splendid palaces were built in old Fez for the rich merchant families. These sumptuous dwellings were ornamented with brilliant mosaics of shimmering blue-and-green tile and were further embellished with seductive arabesques and perfumed ceilings of cedarwood. Their fountained courtyards of imported marble were dazzling.

In a major architectural advance, the Merinids constructed slender minarets of brick design trimmed with pottery mosaic and crowned with lighted towers that were capped with shimmering, golden balls. The new, shining white city of *Fez Jdid* was constructed in 1276 outside the walls of old Fez. Its brownish-red double walls, flanked by square watchtowers, had only a few gates, making it first and foremost a military stronghold. It also served as an administrative residence for the sultan, his family, his court, and his troops. The two halves of the city, now worn and tempered by age, are indistinguishable.

In addition, the Merinids established a series of *madrassas*, residential colleges for religious learning. Architecturally brilliant, these great edifices are freighted with stucco stalactites and elaborately carved wooden screens. By the fourteenth century, Fez had become not only a major center of commerce but one of the shining lights of learning in all of western Islam.

Ninety years ago, a Frenchman, Eugene Aubin, much enamored of the *Fassis*, (as residents of Fez are known), described them this way:

> Fez is a city of sages and merchants, their tongue is quick, their criticisms acute, and their sarcasm mordant. By temperament they are always malcontent…[although] the inhabitants of Fez are always of a more subtle and acute intelligence than the other peoples of the Maghreb.

At the end of the twentieth century, *Fassis* are still regarded by many as arrogant aristocrats, the self-styled intellectual and religious elite of the country. The two imperial cities of Meknès and Fez lie on the plain of Saïs, a low, fertile area protected (and almost totally enclosed) by the Rif and Middle Atlas Mountains. On this plain, well-tended vineyards are tenderly screened from winter winds by protective walls of cypress and eucalyptus. In the fall they produce an abundant harvest of grapes. Morocco is especially celebrated for a particular rose wine known as *gris*. Orchards of apricots, peaches, and plums yield a bountiful supply of fruit. In the center of the plain of Saïs lies the small mountain Jebel Zerhoun. Because of Zerhoun's strong defensive position, the mountain has traditionally served as a haven for refugees from both war and famine. In times past, Berbers from the Rif took up residence on the north side of this mountain. Here they cultivated fig, carob, and other fruit trees and lived among the prickly pears that grow in the mountain's rocky gorges.

Moroccans who inhabit the villages on Jebel Zerhoun have a reputation that belies the tranquillity of the quiet hills. Although they are self-sufficient and pious people, their villages harbor several idiosyncratic religious brotherhoods. One of these fraternal organizations, the Hamadasha, is famed for using dance and music to induce a state of mystical ecstasy. Its members may also perform acts of self-mutilation during their twirling religious trances. The Hamadasha may slash their scalps with knives, drink boiling water, or sit on burning coals. While these practices are now forbidden by law, it is said that they still continue in more clandestine venues.

Jebel Zerhoun is a sacred mountain. The tombs of the Berber saints Sidi Ali and Sidi Ahmed are here. The mountain is also the site of one of the many grottoes across the land that are said to be the home of Aïsha Qandisha, a malevolent female spirit whose feet are in the form of camel hooves. She may appear either as a seductively beautiful and voluptuous woman (hiding her camel's feet under her caftan) or as a dried-up old hag. Men who fall under her spell behave as if possessed. According to local legend, a man will have no defense against the magical powers of this malign spirit unless he plunges a steel knife into the ground while reciting verses from the *Qur'an*.

Built into the steep hillside of the Zerhoun mountain is the quiet village of Moulay Idriss, regarded as one of Islam's most sacred places. Pilgrims travel from all over Morocco to visit its sanctuary and prayer halls, which lead to the holy tomb of Morocco's first legitimate Islamic ruler, Idriss I. Moulay Idriss escaped the wholesale slaughter of his family ordered by the caliph of Baghdad in 786 by fleeing from the Arabian peninsula to Morocco, where he established the first Islamic state. Open only to Muslims, the tomb of Idriss I rests on a catafalque draped with an ornate covering and richly embroidered in gold and silver threads. The cloth was a gift from King Hassan II.

Three hundred families live in this quiet, hillside village. Open only to foot traffic, the streets of Moulay Idriss are crooked and steep. Along these hilly, stepped pathways lined with simple, whitewashed houses, many handsome and ornate eighteenth-century doorways still remain intact, intricately carved and studded with iron.

So hypnotic is the holy atmosphere that even "nonbelievers" tend to speak quietly and behave reverentially while visiting its quiet streets.

The settlement of Meknès, originally known as "Meknès of the Olive Trees," had its beginnings in the ninth century. Zenata Berbers from the Meknassa tribe settled here on the fertile plain of Saïs.

The sequence of rule in Meknès follows the same history as that of the other great cities of Morocco. In the eleventh and twelfth centuries, Meknès passed through the hands of Almoravids and Almohads, and from the thirteenth until the seventeenth centuries it was under the control first of the Merinids and then of the Saadians.

The first Alaouite prince was Moulay Rachid, a descendant of an Arab family that had long resided in the southeastern oasis of the Tafilalt but that could trace its ancestry back to Ali and the Prophet's daughter, Fatima. Rachid seized the throne in 1666. But only a few years later, in 1672, Rachid's younger brother, Moulay Ismail, became sultan. Despite his deserved reputation as a cruel and vicious megalomaniac, many of Moulay Ismail's accomplishments were commendable. He drove the English from Tangier, expelled the Portuguese from their fortresses on the Atlantic coast, captured Senegal, built bridges, and made the roads of Morocco safer for travel. The sultan's military legacy extended to the seventy-six fortresses constructed throughout his empire.

Moulay Ismail's army of 150,000 men included captives from black Africa, Arabia, the Sudan, and Andalusia, and 25,000 Christian slaves. The sultan established black military units that were garrisoned in a series of *kasbahs* throughout southern Morocco. Having restored Morocco's international prestige, he dealt as an equal with both Louis XIV of France and James II of England.

Because the cities of Fez and Marrakesh were both deeply embroiled in seditious rebellions against him early in his reign, the new sultan decided to create his own imperial city at Meknès. The young ruler launched a gigantic building program that extended to thirty palaces and twenty-five miles of triple ramparts. For his standing army of 25,000 black slaves known as the Abids, he ordered stables, exercise fields, enormous garrisons, and granaries. His fanatical and obsessive need for new palaces has earned him comparison with Louis XIV and his palace of Versailles.

But there was a darker side to his display of magnificence. Legend has it that when a starving slave came to Moulay Ismail asking for a crust of bread, the sadistic sultan ordered the slave's teeth to be pulled out, saying, "Now you will have no need for bread." The mad sultan's cruelty knew no bounds: the deaths of hundreds of thousands of slaves were reported during his maniacal building programs. When he was irked by a work slowdown, he personally skewered slaves with a long sword. According to historian Scott O'Connor, "When the slaves died, they were used as building material and immured in the rising walls, their blood mixed with the cement that still holds them together in its grip." Somewhat kinder to animals, Moulay Ismail commanded that the horses that had accompanied him on his pilgrimage to Mecca were never to be ridden again. His many dromedaries were shampooed every other day. Inordinately fond of cats, he kept forty of them, sleek and well-fed, at his palace.

Almost a hundred years ago, French writer Pierre Loti described Meknès with its mosques, minarets, and terraces as "even more imposing than Fez and more solemn — but only a phantom of a town — a mass of ruin and rubbish."

Today, more than three hundred years later, the Alaouite dynasty still rules Morocco. King Hassan II presides over the oldest kingdom in the Muslim world from his necklace of royal palaces, with Meknès's elegant, ornate, imperial buildings among its jewels.

In Meknès, the mausoleum of Moulay Ismail is the only mosque in Morocco open to non-Muslims. A guard stands at the entrance to the main courtyard. As in mosques throughout the world, visitors must remove their shoes before entering.

For seven-year-old Moroccan girls, the twenty-seventh day of Ramadan is a special day of celebration that marks the end of their first day of fasting. At this age, girls are expected to begin to regard the fast, not as a punishment, but as a participation in an important rite of Islam. Girls do not usually engage in regular fasting until they reach puberty, so this introductory observance, coming years earlier, is merely symbolic. Dressed in fancy costumes and elaborate, sparkling dresses (which are often white), their hands are soaked in henna and their eyes are lined with *kohl*. Rouge turns their lips a brilliant red. Delighted with their outfits, they dance in the streets. The little girl pictured here is only four, but she has been permitted to join her big sisters on this special day.

The twenty-seventh day of Ramadan follows a very sacred *Lailat-el-qadr* (night of destiny). On this special and holy occasion, the mosques are all illuminated and Muslims stay up till dawn offering prayers to Allah. On this night, according to the *Qur'an*, the skies opened and the angels came down to earth. In the popular imagination, it has come to be known as "the night of decision," when Allah is predisposed to grant answers to the prayers of the devout.

Near the market area in Sefrou, a spice vendor has set out his offerings in open sacks on the ground. His wares include cumin, peppercorns, paprika, turmeric (which is a root like ginger), and *hilba*, which is used to increase the milk supply in lactating women. The lumpy white rocks are myrrh, a form of incense that is heated in a burner. When warmed to a high temperature, a bubble is formed on the rocks; when the bubble pops, it is regarded as protection against the Evil Eye.

Latticework of straw or bamboo matting allows a bit of filtered light to relieve the gloomy, twilit atmosphere of the medina in Fez. These passageways are known as *les marchés couverts* (covered markets). In Morocco's climate, when summer temperatures reach well above one hundred degrees Fahrenheit, the latticework allows air to circulate while blocking out the sun. The markets of Fez are rich with the mixed aromas of incense, aloe, spices, manure, animal hides, and sawdust. Throughout the *souks* (markets), the rhythms of life are still medieval. There is a vitality in the surging throngs jostling and elbowing their way through the tangle of narrow streets and dark, covered passages.

Overleaf: These supple, buttery-soft goatskins hanging out to dry are suspended from roof terraces that overlook the tanneries of Fez. The skins come from the surefooted goats who scamper down steep hillsides in the Zerhoun hills or nimbly pick their way along high, rocky ridges in the Middle Atlas Mountains. The fresh skins are scraped, and all flesh and hair are removed. The skins are alternately dipped in vats of urine and tanks of sulfuric acid. Finally, the goatskins are lubricated with emulsions of oil and water to lubricate them and to make them supple. The stench of ammonia and slaughtered animals is quite overpowering. The tanneries are manned by guild members who for centuries have formed a complex hierarchy of apprentices and craftsmen. A dynasty of tanners has passed the art on to the next generation. With storklike movements, the tanners step in and out of the gigantic vats, kneading and working a skin with their bare feet, then stepping out to rinse their feet with fresh water. The bright yellow skins will end up in the *souk* to be worked by master craftsmen into *babouches* (heelless slippers).

The ancient, walled city of Fez is the intellectual, religious, and artistic capital of Morocco. Its medina contains the greatest concentration of skilled artisans in the country. Rows of tiny shops line the narrow streets. The minuscule cubicles, often no more than five or six feet wide, have no counters and the floors are raised up several feet off the ground.

Fassi (a citizen of Fez) tailors who work in the city's labyrinth of alleys and narrow, cobbled passageways have a special technique for embroidering and decorating a *djellaba* (hooded robe) with intricate silk braid, or passementerie.

Here, two small boys stand out in the street switching bobbins from hand to hand. The line of braid they are making stretches all the way to the tailor. These children, and thousands of others like them, help their parents after school. All Moroccan children begin public school at six or seven years of age. In the countryside, schools are not uniformly provided past the elementary level. The better students from rural areas enroll in high schools in the towns and cities, where dormitories are provided for those far from home.

Preceding pages: In Meknès, as townsfolk set out on their daily rounds, the soft morning light illuminates the elaborate green-and-blue tile work that ornaments the back of a massive gate. The snowflake pattern is popular in Morocco. The archway leads to the main commercial square of the city. Meknès, despite its present population of a half million, has the feel of a Berber town rather than a cosmopolitan city. A twenty-five-kilometer wall encircles the imperial city.

A group of neighbors in Meknès wait patiently for the day's end in Ramadan's month of obligatory fasting during daylight hours. In the Muslim faith, Ramadan approximates the Christian season of Lent. The month of fasting is one of the pillars of Islam. It is the ninth month of the Islamic lunar year, the month in which the Prophet received the Word of God through the Angel Gabriel. It is a period of penance that predates the birth of the Prophet Mohammed. In ancient times this month of asceticism was so important that it even brought a brief respite from intertribal warfare.

From dawn to sundown each day during the holy month of Ramadan, Muslims must abstain from sex, eating, smoking, and drinking. Not a single drop of water (nor, for the most devout, even saliva) may be swallowed. This fast is particularly taxing when Ramadan falls during Morocco's hot summer.

At the precise moment when the sun sets, a loud siren signals the end of a long and difficult day of abstinence. All town-dwelling Muslims observing Ramadan stop work. While some rush to the closest fast-food shop or café, most go home for a bowl of *harira*, a hearty and nourishing soup made of chick peas, lentils, and beans and often spiced with lemon and tarragon.

Pregnant women, the sick, children, travelers, and warriors are exempt from observing the holy month. Members of the armed services who are actually in battle are also exempt, as are menstruating females. But at the end of Ramadan, menstruating Muslim women customarily add extra days of penance. This practice is called "giving-back fasting."

In the medina of Fez, the area for the dyers' *souk* is on an uneven, narrow cobbled street near the Seffarine Plaza. Skeins of freshly dipped silk and wool drip brightly colored water into the gutters. Passersby must dodge the colorful pools to avoid acquiring newly spotted shoes.

Moroccans seem to pursue lives of constant interchange, finagling and negotiating, promising favors, accruing future debts owed them, and endlessly engaging in a Byzantine series of reciprocal actions.

Professor Lawrence Rosen, the Princeton anthropologist, describes these practices: "If a Moroccan wishes to indicate that he is doing something without any expectation of a possible return, he uses the borrowed French or Spanish term *fabur* (favor). Otherwise, the key term involved is the notion of *haqq* (obligation), which implies that some sort of debt is always created in another by virtue of one's own actions."

In the noisy and crowded *souk* in the old city of Fez there is a boundless profusion of merchandise: false teeth, turtles (believed to be the servants of saints) in small, bamboo cages, *kohl* for accenting the eyes, five-fingered wooden hands to protect against the Evil Eye, cumin, turmeric, and even precious tins of saffron at U.S. $100 a kilo. Plucked chickens seem to shiver nakedly in the window of a poultry shop. They will probably find their way into a chicken *tajine,* an aromatic stew cooked in an earthenware pot and seasoned with pickled lemons, olives, and onions.

Throughout the Middle East henna is commonly used as a body decoration for special events and feast days. Fatima, daughter of the Prophet, was said to be the first person to make henna, but historians suggest that henna was probably pre-Islamic. There is a close connection between folk custom and religion. Henna is used for beautification at weddings, circumcisions, and betrothals. Newborn babies are dipped in it for good luck. Henna is made from a powder extracted from the Lawsonia plant, a privetlike shrub. This particular design was drawn freehand with a sharpened stick dipped in henna. Stencils are used to produce a similar, less artistic, but temporary spiderweb design.

Every transaction in a Moroccan *souk* involves intense and heated bargaining, a skill at which Moroccans excel. The two wool traders shown on the left have completed a successful deal. Resting from their exertions, they are "woolgathering" while they wait for their next customer. The conversion of wool into yarn is controlled by entrepreneurial women called *gezzala*, who take wool on consignment and then farm it out to other women in country households to wash and card. Next in the production line are weavers who turn the yarn into intricately patterned rugs and blankets.

As antidotes to illness, an apothecary in the medina of Sefrou offers a tempting array of prickly porcupines, hawk wings, hares' feet, gazelle horns, and dried bats. The proprietor will also assist in the preparation of charms and love potions. He promises to cure impotence, keep husbands faithful, and make sweethearts jealous.

The pounded and charred head of a hare mixed with salt, butter, and honey may enable a slightly "backward" three-year-old to walk. The blood of a hare mixed with saffron and Moorish ink can create successful love charms. The powder produced from dried, smoked bats is an effective medicine for fever. Porcupines are essential ingredients in a time-honored recipe that promises to increase fertility: "Put a living porcupine in the fire and leave it until it has turned to ashes. Put the ashes in honey and eat for seven days." Hyenas' whiskers burned and then mixed with a husband's coffee will stop his unfortunate habit of beating his wife, while adding a hyena's brain to the evening soup for three days will make a husband more amenable and patient.

Mysterious and exotic, Fez has been described as "the most gorgeously Moorish city of Morocco." It still exudes a distinct medieval flavor. Both exhilarating and confusing, the medina, the oldest part of the city, is rich in mosques, bazaars, tiled courtyards, and jostling crowds. The life of Fez swirls through honeycombed passages, blind turns, secret tunnels, and narrow, often steep streets. Laden with bulging panniers full of unwieldy cargoes of furniture, wool, brass and copper pots, or dyed leather from the tanneries, donkeys and mules clip-clop along tiny passageways. Their drivers shout out the warning cry, *"Baalak, baalak!"* ("Look out, look out," or literally, "Be aware"), forcing pedestrians to flatten themselves against the dusty walls or risk a painful encounter with an inlaid table or a delicately etched samovar.

In the holy town of Moulay Idriss, this graceful, eighteenth-century door frame seems to soar heavenward, enclosing an unusual type of double door bearing two knockers and a complicated hinge in the shape of a trident. Traditionally, the lower knocker was used by members of the family, while the higher knocker was to be used by strangers and foreigners.

The Karouine Mosque in Fez is celebrated throughout North Africa. Within its 270 pillars, the mosque accommodates 23,000 persons, more than Canterbury Cathedral or Notre Dame. Closed to all nonbelievers, the mosque has seventeen doors leading into the medina. The courtyard is a long, rectangular expanse of black-and-white tiles laid out in geometric patterns. A marble fountain at the center of the courtyard is used for the ritual ablutions required of all Muslims before prayer. In the sixteenth century the great historian Leo Africanus observed that on the twenty-seventh day of Ramadan (when the *Qur'an* was dictated to the Prophet by the Angel Gabriel) the great mosque was ablaze with seventeen hundred oil lamps. The giant bronze chandeliers were surrounded by lamps made from melted-down Christian church bells.

Legend has it that in medieval times it was in this holy mosque that a scholar from Fez imparted the knowledge of Arabic numbers and the use of the zero to a pilgrim from France. This pilgrim, who later became a pope, then disseminated the study of mathematics, as well as the Arabic number system, throughout Europe.

The Karouine Mosque is connected with the celebrated Karouine University, which for centuries was the only center of higher learning for Muslims in Morocco.

The *Ulema*, or religious elite of Morocco, maintain that the Karouine has always provided the world's finest teachers of Arabic and of the *Qur'an*.

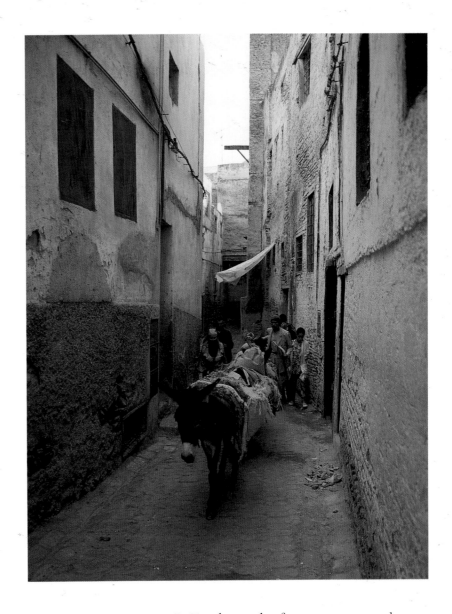

In Fez the tangle of narrow streets and the rhythms of life are still medieval. Donkeys and mules are the primary means of transport for all goods.

Right and overleaf: The courtyard of the Sahrij *Madrassa* (1321–23) in Fez presents a rare haven of peace and tranquillity in the midst of the turbulent and swirling sea of humanity that fills the medina. In this Merinid religious school, intricately carved wooden screens, designed and organized into complicated and sensuous geometric patterns, emphasize the transition from one realm to another. The passage is from light to darkness and from nature to man's constructed world. The openwork screens draw the eye toward an interior space and lead the viewer to seek that which is intended to remain obscure. Square Kufic writing adorns the wooden gate.

Here, the stucco decoration and carved screens are splendid examples of the Islamic mastery of the art of geometric design. It is said that after a few minutes of proper concentration on the repetitive patterns of design, one withdraws inward and achieves a perfect contemplative state. In the same manner, Muslims use prayer beads for concentration and spiritual restoration.

Throughout the Muslim world, *madrassas* provide a quiet retreat for religious study.

For centuries, there was a Moroccan saying that "a sultan's throne is on horseback." Today, the Moroccan monarch still moves about throughout his realm. The reigning king, His Majesty Hassan II, often travels from one to another of his royal palaces in the imperial cities of Fez, Marrakesh, Meknès, and Rabat, accompanied by a large retinue. Wherever the King is in residence becomes the designated capital and imperial city. A new palace is under construction in the southern town of Erfoud.

These modern brass doors open on the King's Palace in Fez. The palace grounds cover one hundred acres and are located in *Fez Jdid* (new Fez), a section of Fez planned by the Merinid rulers in the thirteenth century. In Morocco, it is not unusual for palace complexes to include golf courses as well as elaborate stables.

This hand-loomed blanket was woven in a tiny settlement on the southern slopes of the Middle Atlas Mountains. The woolen blankets are used as bedding, floor coverings, shawls, and even for winnowing barley by tossing it into the air. The heavier grains drop down onto the blanket and the lighter chaff is blown away by the reliable mountain breezes. Berber women use vegetable dyes to color the yarn and then weave the rugs during the long winter months. The Berber women sell the blankets, pocket the money, and are consequently often richer than their husbands. The woven stockpiles are the equivalent of currency or a bank account.

Above the doorway of this Berber woman's home in the Middle Atlas Mountains are white handprints symbolizing the Hand of Fatima. Insurance against the Evil Eye, they are found on walls and doorways throughout Islam. The notion of a malevolent presence expressed as an Evil Eye is commonly accepted throughout the Mediterranean region by Christians and Muslims alike. The Evil Eye symbolizes man's dual nature — the possibility of good or evil in every person. The handprints are usually made by a right hand, so the prints shown here, made by a left hand, are a distinct anomaly.

In Morocco there is constant interchange between country and town. Rural Berbers travel back and forth to sell vegetables and produce, to visit friends and relatives, and to seek jobs in urban areas, but they usually return to their country homes to touch base with the families they have left behind. This woman from the Middle Atlas Mountains has come to Sefrou to sell her small supply of vegetables in the market.

Elaborate tattoos of the kind she bears are rarely seen among the younger generation of Moroccan mountain dwellers. It has been said that facial tattoos serve as a symbolic equivalent to veiling.

Overleaf: North of the imperial cities of Meknès and Fez, flocks of sheep graze among hundreds of olive trees on the lower slopes of Jebel Zerhoun, a small mountain rising over 3,368 feet out of the plain of Saïs.

At Meknès, one of Morocco's imperial cities, a lonely procession of tired columns stands, worn by time and weather. Dandelions, wild daisies, and weeds struggle bravely for survival among eroded pillars and mossy arches. These ruins were once part of a magnificent, colonnaded stable that covered twenty acres and housed the royal cavalry. This grandiose structure was built by Sultan Moulay Ismail, who ruled Morocco from 1672 until his death in 1727.

Adjoining the royal stables were vast granaries, warehouses for food supplies in case of siege. These granaries also held barley and hay for the sultan's 12,000 horses. A remarkable feat of engineering, the granaries were temperature-controlled by an intricate system of water-bearing conduits.

The old city of Fez seems to be ringed by cemeteries. Outside the ancient city walls, the late-afternoon light warms a Muslim graveyard. In the older cemeteries, most headstones bore no name. The persona of the deceased was obliterated. All believers were considered equal in the eyes of Allah. The modern custom of adding names to the gravestones is an urban and middle-class phenomenon. Muslims are always buried with their faces turned toward the holy city of Mecca. By custom, burial must take place on the day of death or before noon of the following day. The body is washed and wrapped in a shroud and placed on a bier. It is carried to a mosque where prayers are offered. The sole prayer for the dead has always been the universal words of devotion said each day by the world's eight hundred million Muslims: "There is no God but Allah and Mohammed is his Prophet."

In the countryside, Berber peasants mark their graves with simple stones. All over Morocco, Muslim families visit the graves of their loved ones on holy days. The visit, which often includes a picnic, is both an outing and a celebration of the life of the departed. A *koubba*, or domed saint's tomb, stands behind the simple, unnamed graves.

163

THE COASTAL PLAIN

Crumbling stone battlements adorn the quaint seaside towns along Morocco's Atlantic coast. They are a daily reminder that in the fifteenth and sixteenth centuries Morocco's history was a continuous saga of siege and domination. The contending powers were chiefly the Spanish and the Portuguese. But a period of stability followed the signing of the Treaty of Fez in 1912, when the northern settlements of Larache and Asilah both came under the control of the Spanish protectorate. To this day, the second language of these towns is more often Spanish than French.

The most picturesque of the coastal settlements—and certainly the one with the most captivating history—is the small city of Essaouira, a two-hour drive west of the imperial city of Marrakesh. This enchanting blue-and-white fishing port (whose name means "little ramparts"), was known for centuries as *Migdol,* the Phoenician word for "lookout tower." As early as the seventh century B.C., Phoenician trading vessels made regular stops at Essaouira. In Roman times, during the provincial reign of Numidian King Juba II, Essaouira was famous for the purple dyes that were extracted from the shellfish dug from local harbor sands. Purple was the symbolic color of imperial Rome.

In the medieval period, Essaouira's bay, facing the Mogador Islands, formed the principal port on the southern Moroccan coast. Here trans-Saharan caravans unloaded their rich and exotic cargoes of ivory, ebony, gold, ostrich plumes, and gum arabic. These treasures were then shipped to England. In return, the English sent back tea, cotton, and Manchester-made, Andalusian-style teapots for the Moroccan trade. During this prosperous period, a clever Moroccan sultan moved skilled Jewish traders from Agadir to Essaouira, where they played an active role as intermediaries with Christians. Until the early twentieth century, in consequence, the Essaouiran Jewish community numbered over nine thousand.

In the sixteenth century King Manuel of Portugal seized Essaouira to further his scheme for controlling the lucrative Moroccan trade, establishing a fort at the water's edge. But a few years later the Saadians, a militant Arab dynasty from the Drâa valley, recaptured Essaouira and Agadir. Today, little remains of the Portuguese battlements.

Further down the coast, a starkly different Morocco exists. For travelers drawn to the hidden mysteries of the medina in Fez—dark, shrouded, medieval, and secret—Casablanca may hold only moderate appeal. Many visitors are dispirited to learn that the American film classic *Casablanca* was not shot in Morocco, nor do its scenes bear any similarity to the city of that name. Those cherishing intense nostalgia for Humphrey Bogart's and Ingrid Bergman's tortured farewells will be sorely disappointed when they encounter the office towers and suburban sprawl of this huge metropolis of four million people.

After Cairo, Casablanca is Africa's second largest city. The heart of this sprawling collection of industrial installations, high-rise office buildings, urban slums, and hotel towers is laid out in European style. Large, open squares, public parks, and wide, straight boulevards flanked with lofty, columnar royal palms reflect the grandiose taste of the

Preceding pages: Much of Morocco's Atlantic coast is protected by forbidding cliffs and jagged, black, volcanic rocks. Near the coastal road from Casablanca to Rabat, a determined fisherman perches on the slippery promontory, casting his line into the foaming surf.

French city planners. The building boom in the 1930s brought battalions of French, Algerian, and Tunisian architects to the city. They left a legacy of white facades, richly ornamented with balconies, columns, wrought iron, stucco balustrades, cedarwood trim, and round cupolas. Some admirable art deco buildings from this period still remain. The streets of the wealthy are lined with glossy-leaved ficus trees, clipped into perfectly rounded, symmetrical shapes. Villas stand almost unseen behind high, white walls, swathed in vines of fuchsia and bougainvillea. In the spring, the scent of orange blossoms perfumes the air.

Casablanca's Atlantic corniche is punctuated with private swim clubs and expensive seafood restaurants. Situated on prime Casablanca real estate, the first McDonald's to appear on the African continent lifts its golden arches toward the sky. In cultural contrast (and directly across the road) is La Cléopatrie, a restaurant decorated in the Scheherazade style, complete with silken hassocks and beaded curtains.

Farther east along the corniche is the newly constructed mosque of Hassan II. This is the westernmost mosque in Islam and surely the most spectacular new building in Morocco. The minaret stands 98 feet taller than the great Pyramid of Cheops and reaches 131 feet higher than the dome of St. Peter's Basilica in Rome. Atop the minaret is a laser beam so powerful that its green rays pointed toward Mecca are visible for twenty miles. Constructed on a filled embankment, the mosque reaches out into the sea, and the billowing waves of the Atlantic can be seen rising and falling beneath a glass floor. This is the fulfillment of a verse in the *Qur'an*: "The throne of god was built on water." For Arabs, the seacoast was considered a final and desperate stopping place for those who had been driven from the rich grazing lands of the interior. Symbolically, then, with the completion of this exquisite shrine, the traditional Moroccan inland culture is now joined to her modern orientation on the Atlantic coast.

In the center of Casablanca, King Hassan II has constructed a resplendent palace, crowned by a huge octagon capped in green tile. Guarding the approach is a pair of cannon resting on stones bearing a carved rosette, symbolizing the Alaouite dynasty. Tall oleanders laden with magenta blossoms line the long processional walkway. Entering the palace reception room, eight gigantic Venetian glass chandeliers sparkle overhead, their shimmering crystal arms edged in the green of Islam and the crimson of royalty. The great arches, the sculptured niches in the carved plaster walls, and *zellije*—tile mosaic friezes in patterns of rose, crimson, black, and seafoam green—are brilliantly illuminated by the great chandeliers. The handsome marble floors are patterned with geometrical designs laid out in six colors. Crimson parasols hang on each side of the great doorway, trimmed with matching tassels and lined with bright yellow silk. Their shafts are made of polished brass and their handles of pure gold. These parasols are the symbol of the royal personage. The tradition of the parasol as an ensign of sovereignty was introduced under Sultan Ahmed El-Mansour (1578–1603), a Saadian ruler. Even in the early twentieth century, sultans in Rabat would ride to Friday prayers in a royal carriage and return on horseback, protected from the sun by a tasseled parasol.

The city of Rabat dates to the third century B.C., when it was a small settlement and port of call for both the Phoenicians and the Carthaginians. In the tenth century it became a *ribat* (fortified monastery) for Muslim warriors engaged in holy wars. Twelfth-century city walls continue to dominate this bustling twentieth-century city. In 1912 French Governor General Louis Lyautey, wary of the unstable politics of towns in the interior, chose Rabat to be the political capital of the French protectorate. The city is a well-ordered and modern metropolis, chock full of embassies, businessmen, and scholars. Fortunately, a few striking monuments from the city's celebrated past still remain.

Only a mile from the well-maintained *ville nouvelle* (new town) of the capital city stands the Chella Necropolis, an unearthly connection with a distant pre-Islamic past. The town of Chella was destroyed by an earthquake in 1755. Now in ruins, the site still evokes exotic pagan beliefs. Above an arch in the crenelated walls, a Kufic inscription reads, "I take refuge in Allah against Satan." A steep stairway then descends through wild gardens of untamed hibiscus, figs, palms, bananas, and morning glories. To the left are ruins of an ancient Roman city under excavation. Nearby stands a ruined Merinid mosque housing the fourteenth-century tomb of Abou El-Hassan, known as the "Black Sultan." To the far left is the tomb of the sultan's concubine, a former Christian slave whose Arabic name means "the light of dawn." It is believed that this mosque contains a trove of buried gold, but one that is jealously guarded by *djinns* (spirits).

A cluster of seven domed tombs of seven saints (five men and two women) stands to the right of the Chella path. These white-domed *koubbas* contain the remains of important saints, their biers draped in dusty green silk. The tombs surround a small, sunken, rock-lined pool fed by a sacred spring. Here pre-Islamic beliefs still hold sway. Sacred black eels slither through the murky water, casting shadowy silhouettes on the rocky bottom. It is said that a queenly eel with long hair and earrings reigns over the watery domain. Barren women come to this quiet, mysterious shrine where they offer hard-boiled eggs to the sinuous, phallic creatures. The eel, in turn, may intercede with ancient deities who will bless these barren supplicants with the gift of children.

As the dominant colonial power, the French always referred to Morocco's coastal plain as "le Maroc utile" (useful Morocco). Yet, before 1912, most of this fertile agricultural area, though blessed with rich soil, was not cultivated. Under the French protectorate, large-scale agriculture was introduced and abundant harvests of fruit and vegetables were exported to European markets. Near the coastal town of Agadir, where the sun shines three hundred days a year, winter melons, strawberries, artichokes, and cut flowers are scientifically grown on a massive scale. Wheat and barley thrive west of Fez, and strawberry plantations have recently been developed south of Larache.

Today, increasingly restless, young males are leaving the farms and moving to the cities searching for work or a more exciting way of life. Half of the Moroccan population remains to work the land. Their average age is fifty, and three-quarters of them are illiterate. For these, the future holds little promise.

In Asilah each August, an "intellectual festival" brings poets, musicians, and graphic artists to the Palace of Raisuni (also known as the House of Tears). Large, abstract murals are painted on exterior walls, often covering the previous year's designs. It is startling to round a corner and come across an enormous wall painted in jarring colors that contrast with the pristine, whitewashed walls of the medina.

At the Café de la Marine in the hilly, Atlantic seaside town of Larache, there is leisure time for coffee or a restorative glass of mint tea. In the late fifteenth century this port town was home to a fleet of corsair galleys that launched surprise raids on the Portuguese and Spanish coasts.

In the first half of the twentieth century, northern Morocco was a Spanish protectorate. As a legacy of the Spanish occupation, restaurants still provide meals of excellent paella, and Spanish-style architecture continues to dominate the town. Harkening back to colonial days, wrought-iron balconies and window grilles cast lacy shadows on the blue-and-white buildings of the main square. There, a central fountain, shimmering with iridescent tiles of Andalusian style, shoots plumes of water into the air.

The *Oudaya* is the old administrative and military quarter of the city of Rabat. Rabat, on the northern Atlantic coast of Morocco, was partly settled by Andalusian Muslims expelled from Spain in the sixteenth and early seventeenth centuries. It has been the political capital of Morocco since 1913. The *kasbah* overlooking the harbor was constructed in the twelfth century to control the estuary below. Inside the fortified walls, pastel and whitewashed buildings graced by blue or green doors and shutters are now inhabited by a mixture of Moroccan and European artists, as well as by the traditional city dwellers.

In the *Oudaya*, the doors of this Andalusian-style house mirror the blue waters below. Rabat and its sister city of Salé are separated by the Bou Regreg River at the point where it flows into the Atlantic. The river's sandbars have always provided a natural and sure defense against penetration by deep-keeled sailing ships. From 1629 to 1666, old Salé was an independent republic of the Bou Regreg corsairs. Pirate ships manned by oarsmen but equipped with sails used Salé as a base for launching forays against the Portuguese coast.

Preceding pages: Forty-five miles south of Tangier lies the port town of Larache. For millennia, the waters off Morocco's northern Atlantic coast have been an abundant fishing ground. As far back as the early days of the Holy Roman Empire, fish caught here were dried, salted, and sent as far away as Rome. Founded in the eighth century during the Arab conquest of Morocco, Larache is today distinctly Spanish in atmosphere. The Spanish captured Larache in the seventeenth century and constructed fortifications overlooking the sea. A favorite hangout for local youth, these battlements are known as the Stork's Castle.

Overleaf: Seagulls scream as they wheel over the ruined sixteenth-century Portuguese battlements of Essaouira. Gigantic waves roll in along the rocky shore, creating small pits in the jagged rocks.

In the coastal town of Asilah, a spontaneous game of after-school soccer often occurs on the quiet streets of the medina. Only thirty kilometers from the much larger city of Tangier, Asilah has become a chic and choice vacation spot for both Moroccans and European visitors. Seaside houses have become desirable real estate and many bear the shiny brass nameplates of foreign owners. A local Berber population continues life unperturbed by the new residents.

Overleaf and following pages: In 1760, the architectural character of Essaouira was shaped by the astute and forward-looking Alaouite sultan Sidi Mohammed Ben-Abdullah. The sultan used a captive French architect to design the crenelated town battlements (the Skala de la Ville), as well as the medina with its arcaded courtyards that form the *souk.* The sultan not only planned the town but also established Essaouira as the central site of exports from North Africa. As a continuing reminder that the town was once a fortress threatened by pirates and European navies, a pair of eighteenth-century cannons stand guard outside the city walls.

In Asilah, as in many parts of Morocco, green
is used alternately with blue on doors and
walls. The blue paint derives its color from
indigo, which is believed to repel insects.

Overleaf: The sea laps at the fifteenth-century Portuguese battlements of yellow stone that enclose the sparkling, white houses of Asilah's medina. Directly below lies the tomb of a local saint, Sidi Mansur, and the blue-and-green tiled tombs of his family. Expatriate American writer Paul Bowles recalls a time when he lived in Asilah in a house that stood at the edge of the sea, "When the weather was rough, the water came crashing against my dining room windows."

The stark contours of the white chimneys in Rabat's *Oudaya* quarter evoke the bleak scenes depicted by the twentieth-century American painter Edward Hopper. The passerby is told in both French and Arabic that this is a garage.

Preceding pages: Today, Essaouira is a quiet fishing town. A fleet of brightly painted boats, pennants flying gaily, departs each morning in search of sardines, filling the quays with a pleasing early-morning bustle of nets and preparation. Sandy beaches offer some of the most protected swimming on Morocco's Atlantic coast. Offshore lies a group of small islands still known collectively as Mogador. Of these islands the twentieth-century French playwright and poet Paul Claudel wrote, "I know of only one castle in which I would care to be locked up. Better to die than surrender the keys. And that is Mogador in Africa."

كراج
GARAGE

Preceding pages: In Rabat's *Oudaya* quarter, a traveling black musician dances into the neighborhood, beating his drum and performing for money. As he twists his head back and forth in a rhythmic, trancelike motion, the tassel on his hat moves in a circle and is silhouetted against white-washed walls. Cowrie shells, a universal talisman, adorn his knitted hat. The man is a *Gnawi*, a descendant of blacks from sub-Saharan Africa. *Gnawi* is derived from the word "Guinea." Some believe that among their many powers is the ability to exorcise evil demons. Other Moroccans are convinced that the *Gnawa* can cure nervous diseases.

In Essaouira, women cluster to enjoy a bit of gossip while they wait for their menfolk to arrive home from a day at sea. Their children scamper across the wide terrace that overlooks the Atlantic Ocean. Sardine fishing has been a lucrative profession in Essaouira since the days of the Phoenicians.

TANGIER AND
THE WESTERN RIF

Tangier blazes like a bright, white star on the northernmost tip of the African continent. According to ancient mythology, the city was founded by the Greek god Antaeus, the son of Poseidon, who named the settlement Tingis after his wife. Known as "The Gateway to Africa," the port of Tangier has always been an object of intense foreign competition. Under the Phoenicians the city became an important trading port. After the fall of Carthage in 146 B.C. it became the capital of the independent kingdom of Mauretania. Then came the Romans, succeeded by Vandals, Byzantines, and Visigoths. In A.D. 705 the Arabs conquered Tangier with a heroic army of Berber troops recently converted to Islam. Strategically located on the Strait of Gibraltar, Tangier was continuously attacked in the fifteenth and sixteenth centuries by Portuguese and Spanish navies.

In the late nineteenth century Tangier became an international mercantile and diplomatic center. Europeans visited the shining white city to enjoy its beaches and the balmy weather, which cools in mid-October when the rainy season begins. Farmers give thanks to Allah for the blessed rain that comes after months of drought. As the first deluge drenches the local produce market in Tangier's teeming medina, grateful farmers and fruit and vegetable growers respond with exuberant shouts and bursts of applause.

In the early twentieth century, rich foreigners built villas on "the mountain" in Tangier, an area overlooking the sea that is in fact a series of hills lush with trees and flowers. Today these posh villas with their shaded terraces and elaborate gardens still represent unattainable opulence to the impoverished population of *Tanjawis*. No foreign visitor seems to come away with neutral feelings about Tangier. The seventeenth-century English writer Samuel Pepys condemned Tangier as an "excrescence of the earth." Two centuries later, Mark Twain called Tangier "that African perdition." But Truman Capote affectionately described Tangier as "that ragamuffin city," and Joseph McPhillips, headmaster of the American School of Tangier (a man deeply devoted to the city, who has made Tangier his home for over thirty years), speaks of it as "impenetrable and contradictory."

In 1923 the Statute of Tangier established the city as an international authority, and Tangier soon became a freewheeling, tax-free, open port. In the central squares, known as the Grand and Petit Soccos, absolutely anything could be bought and sold. Drugs and sex were available everywhere. In its heyday, Tangier was a glittering playground for the international set of expatriate eccentrics, film stars, artists, writers, and poets, as well as for spies, smugglers, and unscrupulous profiteers. In 1956, when Tangier was returned to Morocco, black-market currency exchanges were wiped out, as was most of the export trade in narcotics. Brothels were closed and the international banking center moved to Switzerland.

There seems to be a high degree of transience among those writers who have

---

Preceding pages: Mules and donkeys are tethered for the day at El-Khemis Anjara, a rural area near Tetouan where a market is held each Thursday. A good mule costs U.S. $800. Mules are an essential part of life in northern Morocco. They thresh grain and pull the wooden plows that till the fields. Tough and well-suited as they are to mountain climates, northern Moroccan mules carry huge burdens. A healthy mule can continue to work productively for up to thirty years. Some Moroccan peasants believe that a woman who eats bread made of flour mixed with the charred hoof parings of a mule will become as barren as the mule.

come to Tangier early in their careers. Many commentators have pointed to the pervasive atmosphere of indolence and apathy that makes writing in the city almost impossible. According to Scottish writer Iain Finlayson, writers have found Tangier to be "chaotic, undisciplined, unresolved, and above all, unrealistic. The anteroom of failure, the casualty of despair." American expatriate Paul Bowles, now eighty-four years old, is an exception to the rule. He has lived in Tangier for forty-eight years, and continues to produce distinguished work in both musical composition and the written word.

East of Tangier lie the foothills of the western Rif. The landscape becomes increasingly rugged; it turns into a land of tribal ferocity. Mountains rise abruptly from the Mediterranean coast. The coastline and adjacent mountains afford ideal conditions for smuggling and other illicit activities. To avoid high tariffs, black-market goods ranging from contraband American cigarettes to video recorders, CD players, and other electronic devices pass from Spain into the almost impenetrable Rif on their way across North Africa. Police roadblocks are common. The innocent traveler finds that having his automobile trunk searched becomes a familiar, though annoying, procedure.

In addition to the search for smugglers, the authorities are hunting for *kif*, the raw material that is converted into hashish. The hill terraces of the Rif produce a dense crop of spear-shaped *kif* leaves. *Kif* is smoked openly throughout Morocco, often in the upstairs rooms above cafés. Quiet fishing villages east of Tangier are often fronts for *kif* exports to Europe. The illicit income derived from growing and selling *kif* is estimated at up to two billion dollars a year—money that does not all go into Moroccan pockets.

A curving road runs east from Tangier toward the towns of Chefchaouen (affectionately known as Chaouen) and Tetouan. In the Rif foothills, the rolling countryside is planted with almond, fig, and olive trees. Prickly pears punctuate the edge of the hills, and in the spring mountain lilacs provide brilliant patches of lavender blue.

Berber men on donkeys travel the curving roads. The men, clothed in brown or striped wool *djellabas*, are taciturn. The women, in their lumpy, red-and-white skirts and huge, tasseled sombreros are usually on foot. They stride purposefully along the highway. These bold women do not drop their gaze when strangers pass, but—unlike southern Moroccans—neither do they wave in friendly greeting. They are on their way to a local market, where a day of buying and selling awaits them.

In Morocco, markets are named for the day of the week on which the market is held. In El-Khemis Anjara, north of Tetouan in the Djebala Mountains, hundreds of Berber men and women come together each Thursday for the most important social and economic event of the week. Between seven and eight in the morning, they arrive by donkey, on foot, or by bus. En route to the market, twenty or more buses stop at dozens of tiny settlements to collect their loads of passengers and wares. Lashed to the tops of the buses are rectangular bundles, each wrapped in blue plastic. Openings in the parcels reveal baskets, ropes, vegetables, live roosters, peeping baby chicks, long-eared rabbits, and every variety of spices, nuts, used clothing, and plastic products. Doughnut sellers bind a half-dozen sizzling hot circles of fried dough with bits of green grass or palm.

Well-fed bulls lurch clumsily from the backs of pick-up trucks. A bull will bring the equivalent of U.S. $700 if he is healthy and good at stud. Sheep and goats hobble unsteadily on three legs; the fourth leg is tied up to keep the animals from running away. Here, as at all Moroccan country markets, local butchers slaughter animals on the spot. The butcher shops have a strong odor of entrails and the unmistakable stench of death.

Near the tip of the country lies an important Rifian city, Tetouan, located on the eastern side of northern Morocco. It has easy access to the Mediterranean trade through the wide Hajera River, and lies in a strategic position between the high Rif Mountains to the north and south. (*Tetouan* is a Berber word meaning not only "the spring" or "the source" but also "the female wild boar.")

In 1399 Tetouan was a mountain stronghold fortress and a staging area for Barbary corsairs, who made frequent forays along the Spanish coast. After 1492, when the Christian reconquest of Spain was completed, large numbers of Muslims and Jews crossed the Strait of Gibraltar, settled in Tetouan, and rebuilt the town. *Tetouanis* still consider themselves to be true heirs of the Andalusian culture. They call their blue-and-white city the "Daughter of Granada." In fact, from 1913 until Moroccan independence in 1956, Tetouan remained the capital of the Spanish protectorate.

The rebellious nature of the peoples of the Rif has been celebrated and recorded over centuries. In 1888 traveler Edmondo de Amicis wrote:

> Those Rifans, Berbers by race who have no law beyond their guns and recognize no authority. Audacious pirates, sanguinary bandits, eternal rebels, who inhabit the mountains from the coast of Tetouan.

These fiercely independent tribes refused to be tamed or placed under colonial domination. In 1920 chaos reigned in the Spanish-occupied zone of northern Morocco after a Berber revolt led by the self-titled rebel leader, Emir Abdel Krim, a tribal chieftain who controlled a well-trained cadre of spirited and ferocious warriors from the eastern Rif. His German-made cannon, which he affectionately called "Félipé," was trained on the walls of Tetouan. These wily guerrilla fighters defeated a Spanish army of sixty thousand troops at the battle of Anual. In 1926 Abdel Krim was finally defeated by the superior military power of combined Spanish and French forces who deployed both tanks and aircraft to subdue the Berber dissidents. Rather than face execution by the Spanish, he surrendered to "The Savior of Verdun," Marshal Philippe Pétain. The emir was later exiled to the island of Réunion in the Indian Ocean. Abdel Krim escaped to Egypt in 1947 and in 1958 was awarded the title of National Hero by King Mohammed V for his valiant struggle against the colonial powers of France and Spain. The rebel hero died in 1963 without ever returning to his beloved Rif Mountains.

This Tetouani Berber woman sits sheltered from a heavy rainstorm that is pelting the medina.

Right: Moustapha Freware, age seventy-two, is the most famous government tourist guide in Tangier. He has been at his profession for more than forty-five years.

Signs on a street corner in Tangier point the way to a tailor shop on the left. The street leads to the *Bab el Aassa* (Gate of the Beating). Public beatings and whippings as punishment for theft were commonplace until the early twentieth century.

Overleaf: One of the central gates of Tangier is the *Bab Amrah* (Gate of Rest). Here, weary travelers may stop to refresh themselves. The wall to the left is part of a massive building once officially named York Castle when it was the residence of the English governor general. It is currently owned by Yves Vidal.

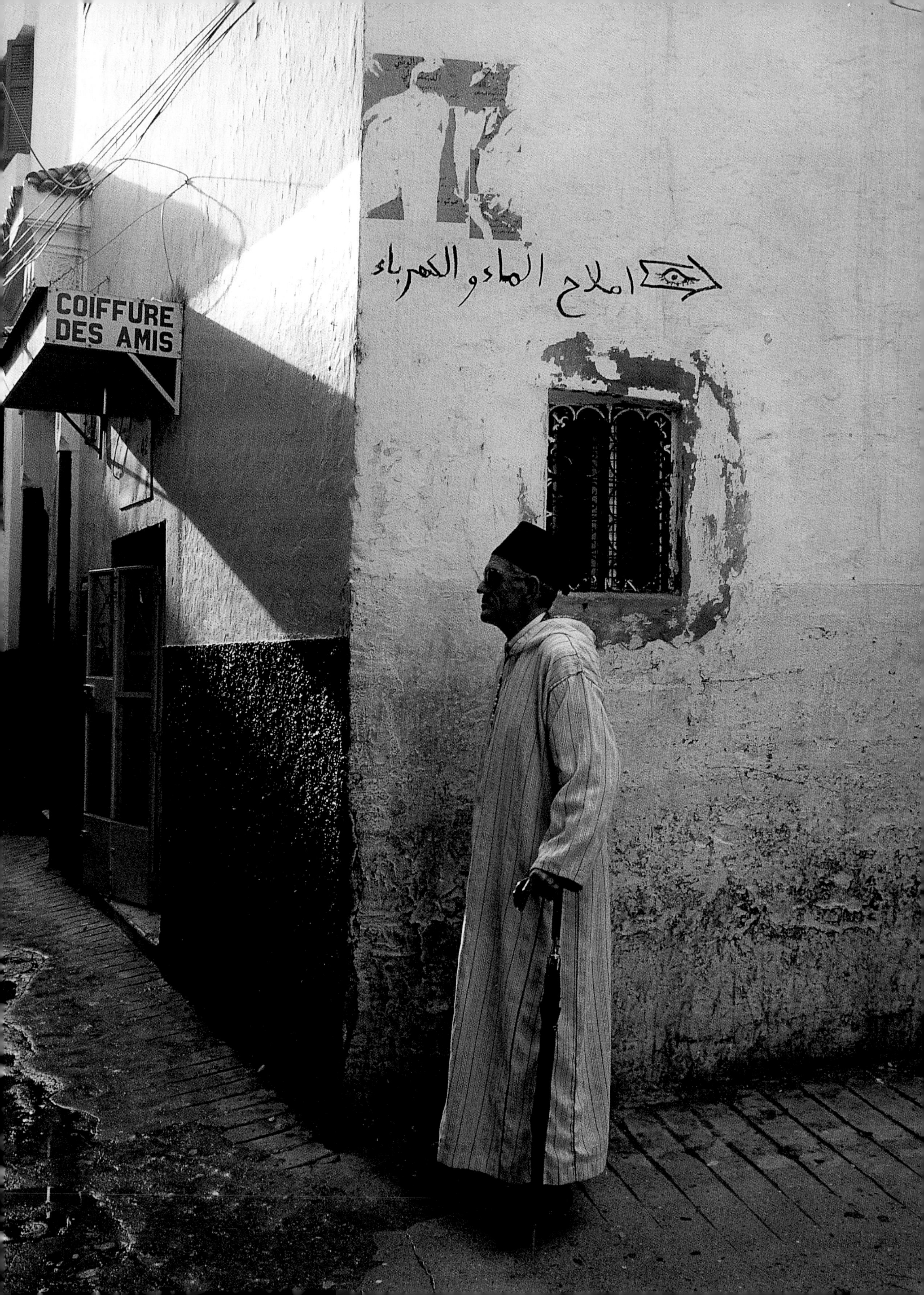
COIFFURE
DES AMIS
اصلاح الماء و الكهرباء

Near Tetouan in El-Khemis Anjara, one area of the Thursday country market is devoted exclusively to the sale of baskets, straw hats, and beautifully woven lengths of rope. These goods are crafted from raffia, a strawlike product made from the dried leaves of the palmetto plant. Raffia is also used to weave the pads that prevent bridles from chafing the faces of donkeys and mules. As every family in the Rif Mountains owns at least one donkey or mule, bridle pads are big sellers. Working and weaving raffia is exclusively women's work, but the men are likely to be the vendors of their wives' products.

Preceding pages: In Tangier, a spectral figure traverses the rain-soaked pavement of the old section of the city. In his recent book, *Tangier: City of the Dream,* Scottish writer Iain Finlayson describes the modern *Tanjawis*: "God-fearing and regular mosque-goers; tight with a *dirham*; given to old saws and sayings; moralistic and fatalistic—believing in signs, portents, and final justice. They are clannish, xenophobic and chauvinistic, suspicious of foreign manners and customs."

Before marriages, birth celebrations, circumcisions, and other ritual occasions, women bind their hands and feet overnight in bandages soaked with henna, a reddish-orange powder. When the wrappings are removed, the henna remains on the skin for many weeks. Henna is believed to have powerful healing properties and to bring favorable blessings, as well as beauty, to the woman who applies it to her body.

The Djebali women of the western Rif dye their heels with henna. When a woman is tightly wrapped in shawls and long skirts, her heels are one of the few visible areas of her body. It is said that a Moroccan husband can recognize his heavily veiled wife by her heels. Some say that a girl's virginity can be determined by inspecting the tendon above her heel.

Preceding pages: Under broad-brimmed hats, these Djebali ladies wear a towel or cloth to cover their hair. Each woman ties a red-and-white handwoven cloth (called a *fouta*) high around her waist. Beneath them, the women tie yards of rope, folded blankets and a *kurzia*, a long woolen shawl or sash. The folds of the *kurzia* create improvised pockets in which the Djebali women hide their money. These mountain women are said to keep all their valuables on their person. The result is a distinctly stout and lumpy profile.

A Rifian woman stops to unpack plastic bags containing wares that she will offer for sale at El-Khemis Anjara (the Thursday market). Unlike other women in Morocco, Berber women of the Djebala region of the western Rif Mountains are tough, independent, aggressive, and uncompromising. They wear large, straw sombreros trimmed with navy blue tassels.

In the small towns of Morocco, there is no conception of public open space. The few parks or large public squares are almost entirely of French origin and design.
In towns and villages, local bakeries serve as the central meeting places where public and private activities are joined. Men gather in coffee houses. For women, a visit to the public baths or the bakery provides a welcome opportunity to leave the house, to see friends, and to glean tidbits of gossip.

In Chaouen, each housewife brings her prepared dough to the baker. Using a long paddle, the baker plunges the round-shaped loaf into the hot oven, where it is cooked for twenty minutes, then returned, hot and ready, to its owner. Old women and children lean against the bakery walls, mentally savoring the village gossip. On Fridays, the local women may also bring in pots of *tajine* to be steamed.

Snow may fall by November in Chaouen and remain on the ground until late February. The women of this mountain community weave heavy cloth from the wool of local sheep. Tailors then create warm *djellabas*, which protect the Berber men from the bitter mountain cold. Tailoring is considered a semi-skilled trade, giving it a medium status in the local hierarchy. Although handicrafts — especially *djellabas* and fine woolen textiles — are still bought throughout a large rural area that surrounds the town, the popularity of running suits and other western-style clothes has hurt the local textile market.

Preceding pages: On a brilliantly sunny morning in the northern countryside, the clothesline is in full sail. Robes and housedresses in vivid colors fly like semaphores, signaling that the rooftop is the woman's private domain, her personal space. She is at the helm. Men are not welcome here.

The market in Chaouen takes place each Thursday in a large, open area near the town center.
Country Berbers bring their produce to sell to townsfolk. Reclining like a pasha, this Chaouen
resident offers oil for sale by the liter. A holy city for hundreds of years, Chaouen was forbidden
territory to Christians, though Jews have lived there for centuries. Before independence,
the citizens of Chaouen relied on business stimulated by the large Spanish garrison billeted in
the town. Now the local economy is dependent on agriculture and milk production.

In the Rif mountain town of Chaouen, as everywhere else in Morocco, community bakeries are busy from dawn to dusk. Typically, housewives or their daughters carry homemade, flat circles of dough to the local baker. Each loaf is stamped with a family identifying mark, placed on bread boards, and carefully covered with a protective cloth. Piles of uncooked loaves outside the bakery await their turn in the wood-fired oven. Baking time is twenty minutes and the charge for baking the loaf is one *dirham* (about eleven cents in U.S. currency).

In late October, the first rays of autumnal sun begin to peek over the tall mountains that give Chaouen its name, "the horns." By December, when the winter sun is low, there is almost no light on the streets before ten in the morning or after three in the afternoon.

Left and above: Children play freely in the steep cobblestone streets of Chaouen. The neighborhood here, as in many Moroccan medinas, functions as a kind of extended family. In mountain towns and villages, children entertain themselves with simple toys made from any available material. A small boy taps out a perfect rhythm on a makeshift tin drum that once contained olive oil. Favorite pastimes are shooting marbles, playing hopscotch, or rolling a hoop with a stick. Small boys also delight in chasing and tormenting chickens.

Chaouen's medina is capped by steeply pitched, red tile roofs capable of withstanding the weight of heavy mountain snow. The walls of aqua, azure, and lavender blue have no right angles. The overall effect of the rounded architecture is reminiscent of fondant, a confection, painted in pastels.

Stairways look as if they have been sprayed with foam. There is a soft, fairyland quality to the narrow streets.

A treasure of Andalusian architecture, the small city called Chefchaouen (now known familiarly as Chaouen) was founded in 1471 by Moulay Ali Ben Rachid. At the end of the fifteenth century, Andalusian Muslims from the kingdom of Granada fled to the town in large numbers and their presence assured its elegant architectural development. Regarded as a holy Muslim city, Christians were forbidden to enter Chaouen's gates until the 1920s. This mountain town is also celebrated for producing many different types of honey, widely believed to cure assorted physical ailments. It is said that the particular honey produced by bees feeding on red button berries is a certain cure for diabetes. For medicinal purposes, former dictator Franco of Spain sent to Chaouen for its marjoram honey.

Preceding pages: Double-handled Berber pots are used to hold buttermilk, oil, or water. While the painted designs look Sub-Saharan in motif, the pots are made in northern Morocco. The black tar at the top of each unglazed pot has been rubbed on the neck to give the water a distinctive, acrid taste.

Berber children play in the shadowed entryways of Chaouen. The Berbers, light-skinned inhabitants of Morocco, have been in North Africa for well over three millennia, perhaps even more. When Phoenician traders landed on the rocky coast of what is now Morocco in 1200 B.C. they came upon a race that worshipped the sun and made sacrifices to the moon. Later, the Phoenicians would conquer these indigenous people.

Most scholars today agree that the Berbers originally came from that part of the Middle East which now includes Jordan, Syria, Palestine, and Lebanon. However, Berber origins continue to be murky. There is no written language, but there are three distinct Berber dialects. Mountain Berbers often cannot understand the speech of Berbers from the desert. There are Berbers with blue eyes and brown eyes and Berbers with curly brown hair and straight blond hair. There are millions of Berbers in Morocco's cities, and there are Berber nomads and semi-nomads who live throughout the craggy mountain ranges of the country. Anthropologists speculate that after a thousand years of intermarriage, at least 85 percent of all Moroccans have some Berber blood.

History of Morocco

12,000 B.C. Early human records were found in eastern Morocco, where human skeletons of the Mechta-Afalou Homo sapiens type were discovered.

1500 B.C The Berbers originated with a people called the Libou who migrated from the east into Morocco and mixed with the indigenous inhabitants. The resulting population, known as Berbers (after the Latin *barbari*, meaning barbarian), came to speak a Hamitic language related to that of ancient Egypt.

1000 B.C. The Phoenicians established settlements on both sides of the Strait of Gibraltar before 1000 B.C., bringing with them skilled artisans, the pottery wheel, an alphabetic writing system, improved weaving, new crops, and iron and metal work. By the fifth century B.C., settlements on the Moroccan coast traded in metal, corn, oil, fish, dyes, and ivory. Carthage was the dominant regional power.

146 B.C. The Roman destruction of Carthage in 146 B.C. brought a new protectorate to the North African shore. In 25 B.C., Juba II was made the king of Mauretania-Tingitana. Mauretania stretched from Morocco to Algeria and was ruled from the two capitals of Volubilis (in Morocco), and Caesarea (Cherchel, in central Algeria).

429 A.D. The Vandals and Byzantines succeeded Roman authority in North Africa when an army of Vandals crossed from Spain to Tangier in 429 and overran the region, ruling for the next century. Byzantine general Belisarius defeated the Vandals in 533, but Byzantines encountered stiff Berber resistance throughout their period of rule.

622 The Rise of Islam began with the birth of the Prophet Mohammed in Mecca in 570. In 622, Mohammed and the fledgling community of Muslims emigrated from Mecca to Medina. This emigration, *hijra*, marks the start of the Islamic calendar. In later times, *hijra* came to signify the rejection of a sinful community in favor of one living in harmony with the moral teachings of Islam. Uqba Ben Nafi led a Muslim Arab army into Morocco in 682, defeating Byzantine and Berber armies. Muslim rulers adopted a policy of religious toleration toward Jewish and Christian communities. The slow process of Islamization began. Soon Arabo-Berber merchants involved in the trans-Saharan gold, ivory, and salt trade were facilitating the dissemination of Islam throughout sahelian Western Africa. Tariq Ben Ziyad led the Muslim conquest of Spain in 711, crossing the Strait of Gibraltar (Djebel Tariq—"Tariq's Mountain") which is named after him. The Muslim forces advanced into France, where they were stopped at the Battle of Poitiers in 732.

788 The Idrissids were descendants of the Prophet Mohammed. Led by Moulay Idriss, they arrived in Morocco after fleeing from persecution in Arabia. Under his son, Idriss II (793-828), many tribes converted to Islam and thereafter claimed descent from the Idrissids. The title they adopted, *Moulay*, means "master" or "sovereign" but implies someone who governs in the name of God. The city of Fez, founded in 789, began to flourish under Idriss II as a center of learning.

921 The Fatimids of Kairouan (Tunisia) were Ismaili Shi'ites who seized Fez from the Idrissids in 921 with the support of the Meknassa Berbers. Both the Umayyads of Spain and the Zenata Berbers soon contested Fatimid control over the region. In 980 the Zirids, a Fatimid sub-dynasty appointed to rule in the Maghreb, broke all ties with their patrons. In retaliation, the Fatimids of Cairo invited the Arabic-speaking Beni Hilal Bedouin tribe to invade Morocco for booty. In the short run, the Hilalian invasion wrought chaos; in the long run it promoted the Arabization of the Berbers.

1060 The Almoravids, led by Abou Bekr and Ben Yasin, advocated a pure Islamic community. From their initial base in Senegal, they overtook and united a politically fragmented Morocco. Ben Yasin's successor, Youssef Ben Tachfin, founded Marrakesh as the Almoravid capital in 1070. In 1086 the Almoravids landed in Spain and their empire stretched over Muslim Spain, the Balearic Islands, the western Sahara, and what is now Morocco and western Algeria. The Almoravids applied Islamic law with rigor. Andalusian culture exerted a pronounced influence on literature, art, and architecture, as can be seen in the great monuments built in the reign of Ali Ben Youssef (1106–1142), namely the Karouine Mosque in Fez, the Ben Youssef Mosque in Marrakesh, and the Tlemcen Mosque in Algeria.

1147 The Almohads overthrew the Almoravids in 1147, calling for religious reform. Ibn Tumart (c. 1076–1130) provided ideological direction to the movement; the settled Masmuda Berbers of the southern Atlas provided the support base. Yet it was actually Ibn Tumart's successor, Abdel Moumen, who defeated the Almoravids, conquering Marrakesh in 1147 and making it his first capital. His son, Yacoub El-Mansour, erected the Koutoubia Mosque on the ruins of the Almoravid palace.

1248 The Merinids were Zenata Berbers who seized Fez from the Almohads in 1248 and established the Merinid dynasty. Intellectual, artistic, and commercial life flourished in their capital at Fez. They are remembered for their architectural contributions: the Chella Necropolis at Rabat; the *madrassas* of Fez, Salé, and Meknès; and mosques, fountains, and *funduqs* (inns) of great beauty. Abou El-Hassan (1331–51) led the way in enlightened patronage, along with his son, Abou Inan (1351–58).

1420 The Wattasids (of the Beni Wattis tribe) took *de facto* control of the seats of government, although European territorial encroachment began with the Portuguese occupation of Ceuta in 1415. *Marabouts* (holy men) in the Moroccan interior began to accumulate wealth and local influence in areas beyond central state control, presenting themselves as the defenders of Islam. The Castilian conquest of Muslim Granada in 1492, followed by the expulsion or religious conversion of Spanish Jews and Muslims, heightened Muslim political consciousness in Morocco. Many Spanish Jews and Muslims settled in Tetouan, which became a base for privateering in the Atlantic.

1554 The Saadians, of the Beni Saad tribe of the Drâa River valley, secured Fez in 1554 after foiling an attempt by the Ottomans of Algiers to restore the Wattasid sultan. From as early as 1511, the Saadians, in collaboration with local *marabouts*, had been working to drive the Portuguese from their Moroccan footholds. In 1542 they succeeded in expelling the Portuguese from Agadir, Safi, and Azemmour. In 1578, at Ksar El-Khebir, Ahmed El-Mansour (r. 1578–02) defeated the Portuguese army (including its king, a Moroccan sultan, and a royal ally) at the Battle of the Three Kings. In 1591 Saadian armies conquered the Songhay Empire and took its capital at Timbuktu, thereby securing the West African gold trade. Commerce was encouraged, a professional army recruited, the Ben Youssef *madrassa* built, and the magnificent El-Badia Palace constructed. This glittering period ended abruptly with the death of Ahmed El-Mansour and the onset of a half century of tribal war.

1668 The Alaouites, a family descended from the Prophet Mohammed through his grandson, Hassan, came from the oasis of Tafilalt to seize power under the leadership of Moulay Rachid in 1666. Rachid was succeeded by his powerful brother, Moulay Ismail (1672–1727), who built towns, bridges, forts, and roads; restored shrines and mosques; facilitated trade; and improved internal security. He established Meknès as the new capital and formed a black slave army of 150,000 (including an elite praetorian guard). He cultivated foreign relations with potentates such as Louis XIV of France and James II of England, at the same time recapturing European-held coastal positions, including Larache and Tangier.

1727 Alaouite retrenchment followed the death of Moulay Ismail in 1727. Taxes went uncollected and troops went unpaid; in response, the disgruntled Abid (slave soldiers) ravaged the land and thereby destabilized the sultanate. The sultans who followed all had to "reconquer" Morocco before ruling it. At best, their authority covered the "Bled El-Makhzen" (land of the government), consisting of the fertile coast, river valleys, and towns; it rarely extended to the "Bled El-Siba" (land of no authority), including the dry plains and mountains. In December 1777 Sultan Sidi Mohammed (1757–1790) became the first head of state to recognize American independence, and in 1786 the two countries signed the first treaty be-

tween the United States and an Arab or African country. Earlier, in 1769, Sidi Mohammed had taken El-Jadida and thereby destroyed the last trace of Portuguese power on the Atlantic coast. At the same time, this sultan encouraged foreign trade, developed the port at Essaouira, and signed treaties with Denmark, Sweden, England, and France. His son, Moulay Sliman (1792–1822), reversed these trade policies and closed the Moroccan interior to European traders.

1830 Imperialism triumphed ascendant as France invaded Algeria in 1830. In Morocco, Sultan Abder Rahman (r. 1822–59) supported the Algerian resistance and its leader, Abdel Kader. But France's defeat of the Moroccan army at the Battle of Isly in 1844 forced the sultan to withhold support for the resistance and turned his own tribes against him. Beginning in the 1830s, Britain promised to protect Morocco from French and Spanish encroachment, and in return secured favorable trading rights. These rights were elaborated in the Anglo-Moroccan Treaty of 1856. After 1844, France considerably expanded her own shipping, mining, and trading activities in Morocco. In 1860 Spain invaded and seized Tetouan, securing her own trade treaty. European economic imperialism continued apace in spite of the reforming efforts of Moulay Hassan (r. 1873–94). Separate Franco-British and Franco-Spanish agreements were signed in 1904 claiming future spheres of influence in eastern and western Morocco, respectively. In 1906, the Act of Algeciras provided for joint Franco-Spanish control of Morocco's police and finances. Tribal resistance to the act served as a pretext for French and Spanish invasion. Sultan Moulay Hafid (r. 1908–12) reluctantly signed the 1912 Treaty of Fez by which France and Spain established protectorates over Morocco with their respective capitals at Rabat and Tetouan. The 1912 treaty afforded a special status to Tangier, the international status of which was affirmed in 1923 and revised in 1945.

1912 The French protectorate under Marshal Louis Lyautey (from 1912 to 1925) implemented policies that better protected Moroccan cultural autonomy than did the harsh French "assimilationist" policies characterizing neighboring Algeria. Even so, the French protectorate was favorable to French firms (notably in the mining industry) and to the French settlers (*colons*) who num-

bered over 325,000 by the 1950s. French policy also sought to divide the Berbers from the Arabic speakers of the plains and major cities. The Spanish protectorate, approximately one-twentieth the size of the French zone, occupied the northern tip of Morocco. It had meager resources and underwent little economic development. Abdel Krim, a Berber chieftain of the Eastern Rif Mountains, launched a successful resistance movement against the Spanish in 1920 before attacking French positions in 1925. In 1926 French forces led by Marshal Philippe Pétain defeated Abdel Krim, who came to be regarded as a Moroccan national hero.

1942 World War II brought "Operation Torch," the first commitment of American troops against Hitler's domination, and General Dwight D. Eisenhower's first major command, beginning a campaign that ended in May 1943 with the ouster of Axis forces from all of northern Africa. In January 1943 Franklin D. Roosevelt and Winston Churchill met in Casablanca to develop ongoing Allied war plans. The encouragement given by Roosevelt and other American officials to the idea of Moroccan independence boosted Moroccan hopes and became a sore point in Franco-American relations. Moroccans who joined the Free French army distinguished themselves in 1945 at the battle of Monte Casino, at other Italian actions, and at the Rhine crossing. During the war, Sultan Sidi Mohammed Ben Youssef protected all 300,000 of his Jewish subjects in Morocco. These years also witnessed the consolidation of the Moroccan nationalist movement, with the sultan as its symbolic cohesive force.

1956–95 Morocco's independence was gained in 1956, after Sultan Sidi Mohammed Ben Youssef, whom the French had deposed and exiled in 1953, returned triumphant to lead the country as King Mohammed V. The king initiated schools, universities, newspapers, public works, and elected assemblies. He developed a strong and centralized state. On his death in 1961, his son, Hassan II, succeeded his father to the throne. Morocco today is a constitutional monarchy that grants broad executive powers to the king. The country's population is estimated at 28 million. Morocco is the world's largest exporter of phosphate rock (used for fertilizers). Its economy also depends upon mineral exports, agricultural exports (notably citrus fruits), and thriving tourism.

Acknowledgments

First and foremost, I wish to express my deep appreciation to two distinguished scholars at Princeton University, Abdellah Hammoudi and John Waterbury. From the beginning of this project Professor Hammoudi has given me expert direction, read parts of my text, and patiently devoted his time and supported me with his concern. He and his wife, Professor Miriam Lowi, have lovingly welcomed me as part of the family into their home in Temara, south of Rabat. Professor Waterbury conceived the idea of a showing of my Moroccan photographs, which were exhibited in 1992 at Princeton University's Woodrow Wilson School under the sponsorship of its School of International Studies and Princeton's Program for Middle Eastern Studies. Professor Waterbury, too, has reviewed parts of my work and saved me from several grievous factual errors. He has been unfailingly generous with his time even when I unpredictably dropped off a chapter on his back porch.

My deep gratitude also to poet, professor, gifted translator, and dear friend Robert Fagles, whose keen eye reviewed a number of captions and chapters of the book. Professor Oleg Grabar of the Institute for Advanced Study shared with me his vast knowledge of Islamic architecture. Institute of Advanced Study Professor of Anthropology Clifford Geertz enthusiastically appraised my photographs of Moroccan Berbers. I am most grateful to them both.

My deep appreciation to Dr. Henry Bienen, formerly Dean of the Woodrow Wilson School, now President of Northwestern University, who has made possible three exhibitions of my work at Princeton University, and to Ruth Miller and Agnes Pearson, who arranged for the logistics of mounting of my Moroccan exhibition. My thanks to Professor Lawrence Rosen of Princeton University. He contributed ideas for captions and patiently commented on all my photographs. Princeton University Professor of Comparative Literature Victor Brombert has generously helped with wise and expert advice and editing on the content and wording of the French translation of this work. I am especially appreciative for his introduction to Nadia Benabid, a wise and subtle woman who has translated my captions and text into lyrical, poetic French. I am deeply grateful to Professor Carl Brown of Princeton University and to Heather Sharkey, a talented graduate student at Princeton, for coming to my aid with a well-researched timeline. Thanks to my travel mate, the irrepressible Martha Vaughn, for her humor and companionship. She shares with me the love of both photography and silver crabs. Warm regards and thanks to my first two *copains*, June and Walter Tower. On the first of my six trips to Morocco they accompanied me and braved an onslaught of fake Tuaregs, aggressive rug dealers, and terrifying mountain passes. In Morocco, my profound thanks to Paul Bowles, brilliant writer and musician, who has honored me by contributing a preface to this volume. Paul introduced me to a colorful and distinguished literary past. I enjoyed many hours of his recollections of the international literary scene at his flat on the Tangier Socco.

Thanks to Joseph McPhillips, head of the American School of Tangier, who entertained me in his exquisite house on the mountain in Tangier and who, when necessary, rescued me by delivering important communications to Paul Bowles. And my thanks also to Blanca Hamri and Karim Benzakour, who are invaluable members of his staff.

In New York, my deepest gratitude to the incredible support staff at 200 West 57th Street, without whose back-breaking efforts this book would never have taken form. My undying appreciation to Adrienne Cannella—always positive, organized, enthusiastic, constantly ready to leap into action to locate a slide, type a caption for the twentieth revision, fax Morocco, or make a trip to the color printer. Her extraordinary memory and organizational skills boggle the mind. To Rochelle Lewis, old friend forever, who has graciously typed, retyped, made phone calls, and been ever loving, resourceful, and always present to help in every way through all my projects past and present. To Elaine Kursch, who has also graciously helped me with color, type, separations, and jacket design, and in reshaping and editing photographs. Annette Gonella has skillfully and diligently aided me in sleuthing for articles, in choosing better colors, in organizing events and invitations, and in a thousand other ways. My deep thanks to Bruce Slater. I was blessed by his virtuosity in database computer research. Irene Tanczyk has most expertly helped me with travel arrangements and preparations. Terese Kreuzer has skillfully copyedited my text and captions with imaginative insights and excellent suggestions. David Pendlebury helped me retrieve important materials on Moroccan lore and culture.

I am grateful for the enthusiastic support and encouragement of Raymond Smith, Joyce Carol Oates, and Walter Lippincott.

My deep appreciation to Daniel Halpern, gifted poet, writer, and supportive friend, for his wise and strategic counsel on many sensitive issues. To Professor Vincent Crapanzano for his sure guidance to life and culture in Imilchil and Aïsha Qandisha. To old friend Eric Laffont who translated some occult works on Berber magic and superstitions, with emphasis on hyenas' whiskers, and who read my French text with skill and insight. Omar Lyettefi has enriched my knowledge of Berber life with his autobiographical accounts of growing up in a small mud village in the Western Rif. My thanks to Guy Horner and Michael Bressler, who continue to be resourceful and expert in hanging my exhibitions. Anne Reeves graciously proffered her artistic vision and sense of scale to my Moroccan exhibition at Princeton University. My appreciation to Alan Keohane, who guided me on my journey to Imilchil in the central High Atlas and then, five months later, accompanied me for four days on my visit to Aremd. My thanks also to Virginia Carr for expediting my communications with Paul Bowles.

A salute to Vanessa Vreeland and her husband, Frederick Vreeland, former United States Ambassador to Morocco. In March of 1992 they graciously opened to me the doors of their neoclassical Moroccan villa. Three years later, I happily renewed my acquaintance with them when we shared lamb and pigeon pie at the King's dinner in Casablanca.

My deepest thanks to my thoughtful editor, Corlies Smith, who has a remarkable gift for subtlety and an ear for the perfect word. He never lacks for wit.

My deep appreciation for the expert talents, guidance, and organizational support of Nan Richardson and Catherine Chermayeff, who spent hundreds of hours picture editing, fitting captions, and expediting the complex arrangements that went into the shaping and production of this book.

My thanks to book designer Tom Walker, whose good humor and keen eye for image make him one of America's most gifted book designers.

To Judith Rulon-Miller, who accompanied me on two journeys, braving freezing cold and collapsing roadways. She kept me sane, helped me organize my thoughts, and supported me with both pup tents and poetry. To Carroll Bever, who educated me in the marvels of moth wings and who traveled with me on the longest conceivable train ride from Marrakesh to Tangier, where little "sleepen" (sic) was done. In 1994 we shared the celebration of the end of Ramadan in the tiny mountain town of Aremd. Both of these women possess generous hearts and subtle insights.

Thanks to Leslie Gelb, who in the fall of 1994 encouraged me to attend the Middle East/North Africa Economic Summit in Casablanca. And thanks also to Judith and Alison Gelb for the memories of our remarkable and speedy journey to Rabat and Fez.

And last, I am ever grateful for the patience, love, and support of my husband, Theodore Cross, without whose constant encouragement there would be no book.

Bibliography

Adams, Harriet Chalmers. "Across French and Spanish Morocco." *The National Geographic Magazine*, March, 1925.

Attik, Mririda n'Ait. *Songs of Mririda: Courtesan of the High Atlas*. Greensboro, N.C.: Unicorn Press, 1974.

Aubin, Eugene. *Morocco of To-Day*. London: J.M. Dent & Co., 1906.

Baker, Christopher P. "The Erg Chebbi, Morocco's Silent Sea of Sand." *Newsday*, Travel Section, November 8, 1992, page 15.

Barbour, Nevill. *Morocco*. Paris: Thames and Hudson, 1965.

Bazin, René. *Charles De Foucauld: Hermit and Explorer*. London: Burns Oates & Washbourne Ltd., 1923.

Beauclerk, Capt. G. *Journey to Marocco*. London: Poole and Edwards, 1828.

Bensusan, S. L., and A.S. Forrest, *Morocco*. London: Adam and Charles Black, 1904.

Bowles, Paul. *The Sheltering Sky*. New York: Random House, 1990.

———. *The Spider's House*. Santa Rosa, Calif.: Black Sparrow Press, 1994.

———. *Their Heads Are Green and Their Hands Are Blue: Scenes from the Non-Christian World*. Hopewell, N.J.: The Ecco Press, 1991.

———. *Without Stopping*. New York: The Ecco Press, 1985.

Brignon, Jean, et al. *Histoire du Maroc*. Casablanca: Librarie Nationale, 1967.

Bruce, Keith. "Desert Heat Blends with an Ethnic Cool." Glasgow: *The Herald*, June 17, 1994, p. 18.

Burns, Tom. "Survey of Morocco." *Financial Times*, November 3, 1993, p. iv.

Caen, Herb. "Journey's End." *The San Francisco Chronicle*, March 8, 1993, p. B1.

Crapanzano, Vincent. *The Hamadsha: A Study in Moroccan Ethnopsychiatry*. Berkeley: University of California Press, 1973.

———. *Tuhami: Portrait of a Moroccan*. Chicago: The University of Chicago Press, 1980.

Daneshkhu, Scheherazade. "Survey of Morocco." *Financial Times*, November 3, 1993, p. iv, p. vi.

Davis, Susan Schaefer. *Patience and Power: Women's Lives in a Moroccan Village*. Rochester, Vermont: Schenkman Books, Inc., 1985.

Dawson, A.J. *Things Seen in Morocco: Being a Bundle of Jottings, Notes, Impressions, Tales and Tributes*. London: Methuen & Co., 1904.

De Amicis, Edmondo. *Morocco: Its People and Places*. Philadelphia: Henry T. Coates & Co., 1897.

De Lens, A.R. *Pratiques des harems marocains: Sorcellerie Medecine Beauté*. Paris: Librairie Orientaliste, Paul Geuthner, 1925.

Epton, Nina. *Saints and Sorcerers: A Moroccan Journey*. London: Cassell, 1958.

Fabricant, Florence. "The Fragrant Food of Morocco." *The New York Times*, Section 5, December 6, 1992, p. 14.

Fernea, Elizabeth Warnock. *A Street in Marrakech*. Garden City, N.Y.: Doubleday & Company, 1975.

Finlayson, Iain. *Tangier: City of the Dream*. London: HarperCollins, 1992.

Fremantle, Anne. *Desert Calling*. New York: Henry Holt and Company, 1949.

Furneaux, Adam. *Abdel Krim: Emir of the Rif*. London: Secker & Warburg, 1967.

Geertz, Clifford. *Islam Observed*. New Haven and London: Yale University Press, 1968.

Geertz, Clifford, Hildred Geertz, and Lawrence Rosen. *Meaning and Order in Moroccan Society: Three Essays in Cultural Analysis*. Cambridge: Cambridge University Press, 1979.

Ghiles, Francis. "Survey of Morocco." *Financial Times*, November 3, 1993, pp. ii, iii, v.

Gloaguen, Philippe. *Le Guide Du Routard, 1994/95 Maroc*. Paris: Hachette, 1994.

Haldane, James. *Trekking Among Moroccan Tribes*. London: Pickering & Inglis Ltd., 1948.

Harter, Hugh A. *Tangier and All That*. Washington: Three Continents Press, 1993.

Hourani, Albert. *A History of the Arab Peoples*. New York: Warner Books, 1991.

Hunt, Carla. *Berber Brides' Fair*. Washington: *The National Geographic Magazine*, January, 1980.

Keeble, Jim. "Travel: Follow Those Camels." *The Daily Telegraph*, June 11, 1994, p. 36.

Keohane, Alan. *The Berbers of Morocco*. London: Hamish Hamilton, 1991.

Knopf Guides. *Morocco*. New York: Alfred A. Knopf, Inc., 1994.

Landau, Rom. *Morocco Independent: Under Mohammed the Fifth*. London: George Allen & Unwin Ltd., 1961.

Laredo, D. Isaac. *Memorias de un viejo tangerino*. Madrid: C. Bermejo, Impresor, 1935.

Le Tourneau, Roger. *Fez in the Age of the Marinides*. Norman: University of Oklahoma Press, 1961.

Lugan, Bernard. *Histoire du Maroc*. Paris: Criterion, 1992.

M'Abun-Nasr, Jamil. *A History of the Maghreb*. London: Cambridge University Press, 1975.

Martin, J., H. Jover, J. Le Coz, G. Maurer, and D. Noin, *Geographie du Maroc*. Paris: Hatier, 1964.

Matthews, Roger. "Survey of Morocco." *Financial Times*, November 3, 1993, p. v.

Matthews, Roger, and Francis Ghiles. "Survey of Morocco." *Financial Times*, November 3, 1993, p. 1.

Meakin, Budgett. *Life in Morocco: And Glimpses Beyond*. London: Chatto & Windus, 1905.

———. *The Moors: A Comprehensive Description*. London: Swan Sonnenschein & Co., 1902.

Mernissi, Fatima. *Dreams of Trespass: Tales of a Harem Girlhood*. Reading: Addison-Wesley Publishing Company, 1994.

Montbard, G. *Among the Moors: Sketches of Oriental Life*. New York: Charles Scribner's Sons, 1894.

Morse, Kitty. "Taste of Travel: Morocco." *Los Angeles Times*, Section 5, October 10, 1993, p. 14.

O'Connor, V.C. Scott. "Morocco Beyond the Grand Atlas." *The National Geographic Magazine*, March, 1932.

Parker, Richard. *A Practical Guide to Islamic Monuments in Morocco*. Charlottesville, Va.: The Baraka Press, 1981.

Pennell, C.R. "The Geography of Piracy: Northern Morocco in the Mid-Nineteenth Century." *Journal of Historical Geography*, vol. 20, no. 3, 1994.

Pierce, Andrew. "Travelling by Atlas." *The Times (of London)*, Features Section, July 3, 1933.

Porch, Douglas. *The Conquest of Morocco*. New York: Fromm International Publishing Corporation, 1986.

Rabaté, Marie-Rose. *Les Beaux Moussems du Maroc: Imilchil*. Paris: Maroc Editions, 1970.

Rosen, Lawrence. *Bargaining For Reality: The Construction of Social Relations in a Muslim Community*. Chicago: The University of Chicago Press, 1984.

Shor, Jean and Franc. "From Sea to Sahara in French Morocco." *The National Geographic Magazine*, February, 1955.

Stannard, Dorothy, ed. *Insight Guides: Morocco*. Hong King: APA Publications, 1990.

Stuart, Graham H. *The International City of Tangier*. Stanford: Stanford University Press, 1931.

Thomson, Joseph. *Travels of the Atlas and Southern Morocco: A Narrative of Exploration*. New York: Longmans, Green, And Co., 1889.

Vaidon, Lawdom. *Tangier: A Different Way*. Metuchen N.J.: The Scarecrow Press, Inc., 1977.

Wayne, Scott. *Adventuring in North Africa*. San Francisco: Sierra Club Books, 1991.

Westbrooke, John. "The Desert Is Waiting." *Financial Times*, August 20, 1994, Travel Section, p. xii.

Westermarck, Edward. *Ritual and Belief in Morocco*. London: Macmillan and Co., Ltd, 1926.

Wharton, Edith. *In Morocco*. New York: Charles Scribner's Sons, 1920.

Willcox, Faith Mellen. *In Morocco*. New York: Harcourt Brace Jovanovich, Inc., 1971.

Wright, Thomas E. *Into the Moorish World*. London: Robert Hale, 1972.

Index